Beautiful art thou, Pentillie, rising o'er the flood
That round thy foot, involved as the folds
Of the sleek serpent, leads a mazy course,
As though it were a pity soon to steal
the voyager from scenes so passing fair

Carrington, as quoted in Lake

This introduction to the history of Pentillie Castle would not have been possible without the help, information and pictures provided by Mr and Mrs Edward Coryton, their family and by many others. Thanks are due to them for their assistance, advice and the use, with permission, of their own material. We take responsibility, however, for all conclusions and opinions, which cannot be laid at the door of these kind people.

ISBN 978-0-9555511-4-7

Pentillie Castle

An introduction to the history, architecture and
eccentric owners of Pentillie Castle

Stephen Tyrrell

Contents

Introduction

Pentillie Castle is famous for its dramatic position high above the river Tamar. Described as an 'elegant and beautifully situated mansion on a commanding eminence above the river', it has a mystique as magnificent from the river but also private, with acres of garden, valleys, park and woodland.

To the north is a partly hidden three storey tower on the top of a hill, which is the mausoleum of the castle's builder, Sir James Tillie.

Not only does the castle's position mean that it's been admired for some 300 years but 'wondrous stories' have accumulated to create a curious respect and reputation.

Pentillie Castle was the creation of one man, Sir James Tillie. It was never actually a castle but built as a country house intended to give Sir James status and as the foundation of a family dynasty he still hoped to found. Sir James Tillie married into the Coryton family, who still live in the building that was part of Sir James Tillie's original 'palace'.

This 'palace', much rebuilt over the last 300 years, is now going through a period of restoration and new energy.

Pentillie Castle has gardens of about 55 acres and a parkland landscape with a further 200 acres. The gardens are the site of one of the early gardens of Cornwall. Not only can Sir James Tillie's designs still be traced, but later alterations were designed by Humphrey Repton, Lewis Kennedy and Victorian and Edwardian plant collectors. The garden, described around 1820 as one of the most important in the county, is now being restored. It promises to be one of the more fascinating and interesting great gardens of the south west.

Pentillie Castle therefore provides dramatic, romantic and scenic landscapes, combined with a fascinating architectural history and important, interesting gardens.

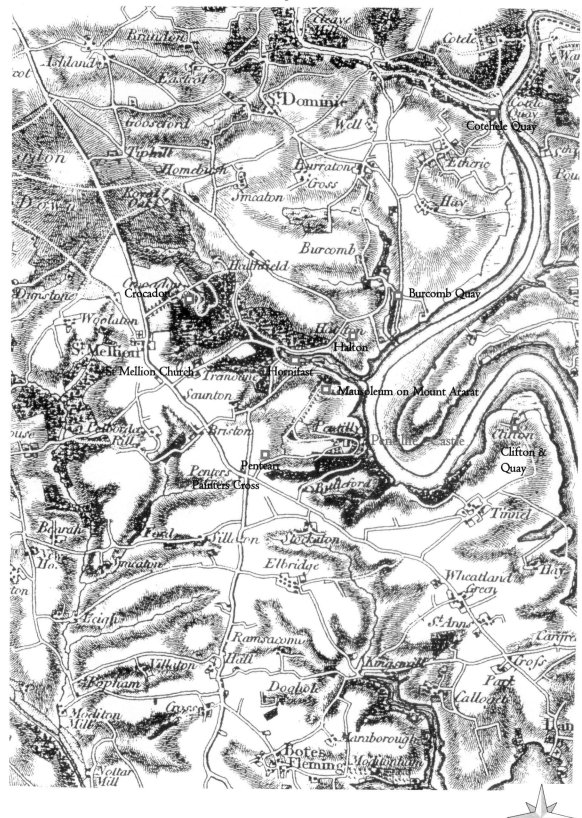

Cotehele Quay

Burcomb Quay

Crocadon

Halton

St Mellion Church

Hornifast

Mausoleum on Mount Ararat

Clifton & Quay

Pentean
Painters Cross

Based on 1809 ordnance survey
Not to scale

Site and Early History

Pentillie is on the east side of a rectangle of land between the rivers Tamar and Lynher, five miles north west of Plymouth.

This was reasonably good agricultural land where the rivers had made possible both habitation and trade around the estuary and its inlets. Landing places and quays were possible up the many inlets of the estuary, and quays can still be found, as at Burcomb, some way inland.

This area of farms was east of what might be called the main lands of surviving Celtic Cornwall. There are early barrows and defended hill forts, but this part of Cornwall is not one that has had much archaeological research.
This area, defined by the hamlets, quays and many rivers and inlets, may have been in the control of those who lived at Cadson Bury Fort, just south-west of Callington, below which was built the great house of Newton Ferrers.

Three parishes, Pillaton, St Mellion and Landulph, meet close to Paynters Cross, which was once said to be one of only two hamlets in the parish of Pillaton. This important crossroads was where met the roads from Saltash to Callington and from Pillaton to Cargreen. There is a possible Iron Age fort at the top of Paynters Cross; field layouts suggest another one on the next ridge north.

The most important sites for the last 2,000 years have been those associated with trade and landing places. Landing places, and later quays were in use at Cotehele, Burcomb, Halton, Hornifast, Pentearr, Clifton and many other inlets where boats could be drawn up at high tide.

Pentillie Castle itself is built on a distinctive hill but no traces of Iron Age fortifications have been found. It seems likely that any early habitations are associated more with the head of the little stream to the immediate south-west of Pentillie.

Paynters Cross was so called because it was the crossroads by Pentearr, an important farm or building just east of the crossroads. Variously spelt as *Penters* or *Pentearr*, this is similar to the not uncommon name *Pentire*, usually meaning a 'house by the headland'.
Pentearr is still shown as a house of substance on the Gascoigne map of 1690.
The family who had lived there must have fallen on hard times early in the 17thC, since such documents as we have show that the holding had been split up amongst numerous different owners and tenants. Even the hearth tax records for 1662/4 suggest that there was no sizeable holding which remained identifiable with Pentearr.

Sir James Tillie is thought to have bought Pentearr around 1680, and then purchased piecemeal the various parts of the holding. These included *'Penters Park alias Leribeaton'* and *'Penters in Pillaton'* and *'Penchaufour Penters and Penters Cross'*, which last is a duplication in two languages of the same phrase.

Early writers tried to find a connection between the name Pentillie and the Cornish language and early place names. I do not think this exists. The name celebrates that of Sir James Tillie, was chosen by him, and would mean therefore,

'The Tillie Headland'.

A family tree showing the Coryton and Tillie families
1500-1800

The Coryton Family tree starts with the marriage of Jeffery Coryton, from Coryton in Devon, who marries Isolde, the heress of John Ferrars of West Newton around 1242.
The last review of the early pedigree was carried out in 'The Visitation of Cornwall' circa 1620.
Many entries have been omitted to improve clarity
The Coryton line is shown in red.
The Tillie line is shown in blue.
Details of the family tree for the period 1800 to the present are inside the front cover.

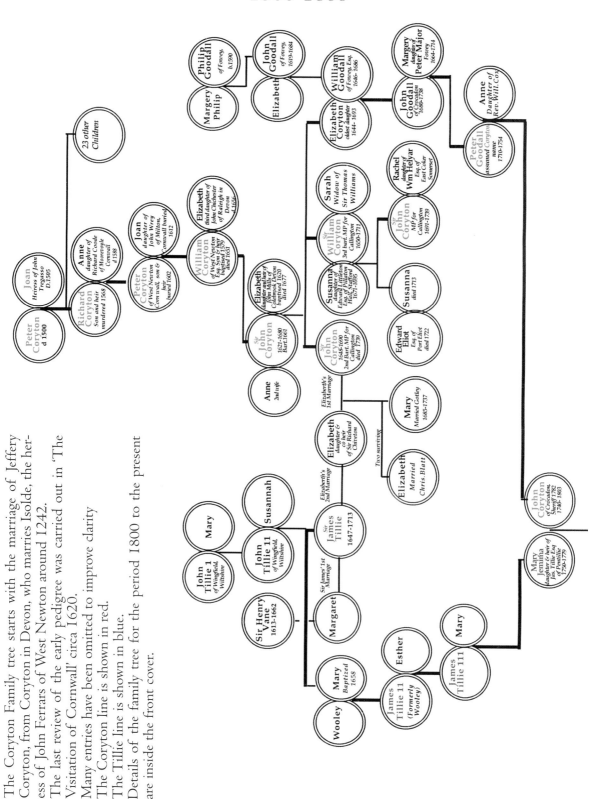

The Early Corytons (1500-1800)
and a famous murder.

Pentillie Castle has always been connected with the Coryton family. The original builder of the house, Sir James Tillie, had acted as lawyer for the family, and had married a Coryton widow.

The Corytons were originally from Coryton in Devon. Good marriages and fortune built up their assets so that they became extensive landowners in Devon. Around 1314 Jeffery Coryton married Isolde de Ferrers and gained what was then called West Newton (or West Newton Ferrers) in Cornwall, so called to differentiate it from Newton Ferrers in Devon.

From 1314 the Corytons continued to accumulate land and wealth, not only by negotiation or purchase but also by further marriages. The house at Newton Ferrers became their principal residence.

The Corytons of West Newton Ferrers were Sheriffs, Deputy Lieutenants of Cornwall, MPs and prominent and respectable citizens.

The Peter Coryton who died in 1500, and is remembered in a brass in St Mellion Church, was famous for having 24 children, one of whom is said to have been the murdered Richard Coryton.

The Murder of Richard Coryton

During the 1550s Richard Coryton was the head of the family and had three sons. Richard was a tyrant at home and refused to allow his son and heir Peter to marry Jane Wrey, the lady he admired. When Peter refused to give in, Richard flew into a great temper and swore to disinherit his eldest son in favour of the second born.

Peter was in London in attendance at court, and in 1564, the father decided to visit London to carry out the dis-inheritance.

However, the evening before Richard was due to leave for London, he was attacked by two men, and his throat was cut.

The two men were caught and, in the spirit of the Wild West, brought before the sheriff, a Mr Trevanion, in Launceston.

Unfortunately, the sheriff knew too much of the family disagreements, or perhaps he had an axe to grind. Peter had not only been unpopular at home, but also with his tenants and the gentry of the area. In any event the sheriff jumped to the conclusion that the murder had been arranged by Peter, from London. He 'persuaded' the two villains to agree that this was the case, even hinting at a pardon if they would confirm they were hired villains. Since Peter was in London, the accused were sent to confront him there. They were no sooner in London than they changed their evidence.

At this point, the story imitates a court-room drama, with an investigation carried out by the Lord Mayor and Aldermen of London.

They arranged for an examination to be carried out by a clerk, who questioned the two men, one of whom was now on his death bed.

Further evidence of interrogation was provided at length by two parsons and by the gaoler.

The story is written in great detail in the report of May 1566, *"Evidence concerning the murder of Mr Coryton"* a copy of which was in the Pentillie papers. The pages of detail and conversations prove a fascinating read. The villains, one of whom was dying, swore that the murder had had nothing to do with Peter 'Currington' (*Coryton*), and that they had been persuaded to give false testimony by the sheriff. The surviving murderer was sent back to Launceston and hanged.

Eighty years later, after decades of contention, the case was revived by John Coryton, a descendant of the younger son of the family. John believed his branch of the family should have inherited the entire Coryton estate, because of Peter's alleged guilt, because of Richard's intention to disinherit his heir, and also because the brother and family of Peter's affianced wife were near the scene of the murder, acting in a suspicious manner and 'with a black box'.

Despite the allegations, and suspicions, John got nowhere and lost the case.

The story has fascinated readers for 450 years, and still reads like a populist melodrama.

William Coryton
A memorial in St Mellion Church

William Coryton 1579-1651

The Corytons had always played a role in county and sometimes in national affairs, as MPs, court officers and officials. One of the most famous was William Coryton, son and heir of that Peter who had been accused of murdering his father. William was Vice-warden of the Stannaries of Cornwall and also an MP. He was one of those who, with Pym, Sir John Eliot and John Hampden, advocated the Petition of Right and prerogative of Parliament. He was one of the three who forcibly detained the speaker in his chair. He lost his offices and was three times imprisoned.
William was a man of principle, but fought for the king as a Colonel, although later he did a deal with parliamentarians to secure his estates. William Coryton, although concerned with principle, was also pragmatic and a practical politician. He died in 1651 and is remembered by a stunning memorial in St Mellion church.

His son, John Coryton (1621-1680) who had also been a royalist Colonel, was appointed a 'Gentleman of the Privy Chamber' and created a baronet in 1662.

Sir John (or William) Coryton 'temp Charles I'
by Cornelius Jansen

Sir John Coryton (1621-1680) was therefore the first baronet. He was succeeded by his heir, another Sir John. The first Sir John also had a daughter, named Elizabeth, who married a William Goodall, and she is important because the estate eventually reverted to her heirs.

Sir John Coryton of Newton Ferrers

The second Sir John Coryton (1648-1690) was the first to drop the title 'of Coryton and Newton Ferrers', and describe himself as only 'of Newton Ferrers', suggesting that lands in Devon were now of less importance.
 Sir John is of importance to Pentillie because his wife Lady Elizabeth was a daughter of the rich and influential Sir Richard Chiverton, who had not only been Lord Mayor of London, but also Sheriff

of Cornwall. She had brought a rich dowry with her, which remained hers on her husband's death. Sir John and Elizabeth had no male heir, and when he died aged only 42 the estate was inherited by his brother Sir William Coryton.

Sir James Tillie and the Corytons.

Sir James Tillie, the builder of Pentillie Castle, was first involved with the Corytons as a lawyer, practising from the Temple in London. He had helped Sir John Coryton with many deeds, acted as witness and indeed acted for him in various matters. He was also a trustee for settlements made by Sir John.

At some time before the mid 1680s he had bought some property, including Pentearr, which formed the core of what is now Pentillie Castle. It is at this stage that all readers have to take a deep breath because the history of the Coryton and the Tillie families and the residences of the Coryton family become entangled and confused, not only by lawsuits but also by changes of name.

The first close connection was when Sir James Tillie, following the death of Sir John Coryton II in 1690 and after a two year gap, married his widow Elizabeth.

Although this was Sir James Tillie's second wife, he died without children from either marriage.

James Tillie the second (formerly Wooley)

Sir James Tillie left Pentillie to his nephew, James Wooley, on the condition that he change his name from Wooley to Tillie.

James Tillie II was Sheriff of Cornwall in 1734.

James Tillie the third

His son, the third James Tillie, therefore took over at Pentillie.

Then, in an act which would seem unlikely even in a novel, the third James Tillie's daughter, Mary Jemima, married back into the Coryton family.

Their son, John Tillie Coryton (1773-1843), thereby inherited both Pentillie and Crocadon, only moving to Pentillie on the death of his widowed mother.

James Tillie
W Vetelois 1750

Mary, Mrs James Tillie
W Vetelois 1750

Sir William Coryton c 1690

Susanna, Wife to Sir William Coryton c 1690

When the second Sir John Coryton died in 1690, his brother, Sir William Coryton inherited the estates of Newton Ferrers and the Corytons.
It is Sir William who is credited with building the magnificent new mansion at Newton Ferrers.

In addition, in 1704, Sir William bought the towered mansion of Crocadon, by St Mellion church, a house which becomes important in the story of the family. It is still within the estate.

Newton Ferrers by Edmund Prideaux 1716

Newton Ferrers was built between 1685 and 1701. (The stable block has a date stone of 1688, and gate piers bear the dates 1688 and 1695). Presumably started by the second Sir John and finished by Sir William - the building accounts are dated between 1695 and 1701- it was built in front and to the east of the old house. Pevsner described it as the earliest Cornish mansion of classical design. It was intended to sit in an extensive formal landscape of terraces, ornaments and gardens and some terraces were laid out 'by an italian'. Burnt in 1940, the house was restored by new owners in the 1990s.

Sir William married twice, the second time to an elderly but rich widow, of whom the commentators of the time wrote:

> Refues noe women nere soe old
> Whose marriage bringeth store of gold.

This widow was so rich that after Sir William's death she married yet again.

Sir William's will, dated 1711, is interesting not only because it throws light on his friendships, his servants, his life and habits, but also because the absence of reference to Sir James Tillie, or to any ancient dispute or dislike, suggests that much of the later scandal about relations between the two families had been invented. Sir James Tillie had been his steward, had acted for his brother and married his brother's wife. There is no suggestion that Sir James Tillie had 'acquired' property from the Corytons.

William had already settled everything on his son when he had first married.

I leave behind me in cash and unquestionable debts on good securitys a much greater personal estate than will pay and satisfy the same with a considerable overplus'.

This was despite the cost of rebuilding Newton Ferrers. He recognised that this, like many building works then and since, had not been efficient, and so left to *'Rich. Smith, who has long served me'*, the considerable sum of £200 (on general release given by him) including debts he owes his master through negligence in accounts, ...'especially in the matter and con-

cern of my new building which was as it seems an undertaking too hard for him....'
He also left Richard Smith the *'clothes both linen and woollen hats and perriwigs'*, and the *'little black mare he usually rode on'*.

Sir William's second wife did well getting (but only when she had released her dowry) a list of furniture and jewellery, the *'broad pieces of gold, money she has saved'* and the *'best chariot, harness, coach horses, gelding or mares, with the grey gelding she usually rides on'*.
If the wife did not want to live at *Newton* with her stepson then she could live at Crocadon as long as she remained a widow.
William had also emphasised to his son and the children of his first marriage that he *'desires affectionate duty and respect from children to his wife.'*

Finally, with generous bequests to servants and many substantial gifts 'for mourning', and after setting up complex trusts for his son (who remained under trustees until he was 27 years old), he requested that he be buried in St Mellion Church, in a funeral 'not to cost more than £50.'

He directed that the brass of his ancestors with their four and twenty children should be resited to a position over the family pew and that in its place a monument to the testator and his wife *'like granfather's'* was to be set up. These changes can still be seen in St Mellion church today.

Sir John Coryton, 4th baronet (1691-1739)

Sir William was succeeded by his son, Sir John Coryton, 4th baronet. (1691-1739).
Sir John the 4th married Rachel Helyar, but died without an heir and the baronetcy died with him.

The estate went to descendants of his grandfather's daughter, Elizabeth, who you, with a wet cloth over your head, will remember had married William Goodall.

It was therefore the grandson of the second Sir John's sister Elizabeth who gained title to the Coryton estates. He didn't have the name Coryton, being called Goodall, but had to change his name in order to inherit.

To add to the confusion, Sir John Coryton the 4th had married a girl from a rich family, the Hellyars. Not only were there disagreements about dowries and settlements, but the Hellyars claimed much of what had been seen as the Coryton estate, resulting in a difficult law suit which lasted from 1740 to 1772.
Although the Goodall connection had brought some lands, the legal dispute damaged the Coryton inheritance. They never lived at the mansion of Newton Ferrers again, and in 1839 it was sold. In the 19th, even the 20th century, the Hellyars had some claim to Coryton lands.
The widow (formerly Hellyar) continued to live at the main house, Newton Ferrers, and that is why for a time the next generation lived at Crocadon.

Peter Coryton, 1710-1754
& John Coryton, 1740-1803

Peter Coryton (previously Goodall) inherited the Coryton estates in 1739. We imagine that the lives of him and his son, John Coryton (1740-1803), were blighted by court action and financial difficulties.

However, it was this John Coryton who married into the Tillie (formerly Wooley) family. His wife was Mary Jemima Tillie, who brought Pentillie Castle to the Coryton family.

John and Mary Jemima were suceeded in their turn by John Tillie Coryton who, in the year of his father's death, married Elizabeth Leveson Gower.

It was John Tillie Coryton who, moving from Crocadon after his father's death, rebuilt Pentillie Castle.

It was only when that son finally left Crocadon and came back to extend and alter the house at Pentillie, that the two families of Tillie and Coryton could finally be said to be settled.

The family's life from 1800 on is reviewed in later sections. It is clear, however, that for some three hundred years the life of the Coryton and Tillie families had been one of rise and fall, of property gains and losses, of good marriages, family disputes and endless legal actions.

There is plenty of material here for a string of racey historical novels.

John Coryton 1769
Attrib: Sir Joshua Reynolds

Mrs John Coryton 1778
Formerly Mary Jemima Tillie

John Coryton in later life
After Romney

Sir James Tillie 1647-1713

An Ambitious Eccentric

'It is certain that Mr Tillie was one of those persons, most justly esteemed, who advance them-selves in the world without being beholden in any considerable degree to their ancestors'.

(Davies Gilbert 1838)

James Tillie is a man of whom it is difficult to get a clear picture.

His death and mausoleum became the subject of much gossipy speculation. The lack of surviving direct family, or of family who knew him well, meant there were no advocates to counter the wilder stories of his life and death.

One notable culprit was the unreliable historian, Hals, who wrote at length only fifteen years or so after Sir James Tillie's death. He described him, with scorn, as the son of a labourer and a man who was little more than a thief, alleging that his steward, a Mr Eliot, and a confederate, Mr Popjoye, were found guilty of making counterfeit money. He alleged that Sir James had robbed his former client, Sir John Coryton, perhaps poisoned Sir John, and stolen his wife and lands. Finally, he suggested that in his new house at Pentillie Castle, he:

liveth in much pleasure and content in this place, honoured of some, loved of none, admiring himself for the bulk of his riches and the arts and contrivances by which he got it, some of which were altogether unlawful.

He also exaggerated the story of his death and the instructions for his funeral. These dramatic tales caught the imagination, particularly the belief that his decaying body remained strapped to his chair, looking over the Tamar, and awaiting resurrection. It is such stories as these that have been remembered over the years.

The truth is more prosaic.

Sir James Tillie had been born into a respectable family in Wiltshire, many of whom were merchants based in Bristol. Joseph Tillie, MP for Exeter in 1695, may also have been of the same family. Although it is clear that Sir James had hoped to

start his own dynasty, he carefully provided not only for his eventual heir, a nephew, but made provision for other members of his Wiltshire family.

The Tillie family were from Wingfield, Wiltshire, where they were described as gentlemen. In 1687, in memory of his father, and perhaps to boast of his recent knighthood, Sir James erected in the church a monument to *'the memory of his ancestors'*, listing their tombs and details. In 1695, and to *retain an attachment to the original home of his ancestors*, he bought an estate in Wingfield called *Belle-Cour*, which remained in the Tillie family until about 1828. At Belle-Cour too it was reported that he had built a new house.

'There was till lately a house upon it, which bore evident marks of that singularity of character which discovered itself upon other occasions'.

Gentlemen's Magazine: 1791

We can only assume that James Tillie went to London in his early twenties, and studied to become a lawyer. He later had a reputation as a good fellow and enjoyable company. Judging from his statues, he must have been a short man, and presumably a man with much ambition and self importance. The earliest picture shows a young man in fashionable dress, described in adulatory terms:

Ce' que Mars et venus, Minerve ont de parfait,
Brave Jacques Tilli se voit dans ton portrait

This extravagant inscription translates roughly as: *He who the gods of war, love and wisdom consider perfection, can be seen by the brave Jacques Tilli, in his own portrait.*

There are few who could accept such flattery nowadays. The portrait was done when James Tillie was a young man. Is it possible he had spent time on the continent?

Of more interest is the legal work, which he carried out from the 1670s onwards. He is found as the first witness on documents, which he may himself have drawn up. He is referred to as active in many law suits, although it is likely that this is for clients, rather than on his own account.

He acquires clients in different and distant parts of the country, and also acquires property in different parts. These included an estate in Durham, part of his first wife's dowry, which he did not sell until he was able to buy more land around Pentillie after 1700.

His fortunes were probably assisted by his first marriage, which was to Margaret, a daughter of Sir Henry Vane.

Sir Henry Vane (the younger) had been one of the great figures of mid 17thC England.

After time as a diplomat for Charles I, he had helped establish the puritan colony of Massachusetts, and was elected its Governor in 1636. It was during this Governorship that Harvard College was founded. The owner of Raby Castle, Vane had spent much of the Protectorate in retreat. Respected as a man of influence and of principle, he was only executed when his previous pardon was retracted by Charles II who, following his skilful defence in support of the rights of Parliament, thought that Vane was 'too dangerous a man to let live'.

The family of Sir Henry Vane, though famous and respected, were therefore going through a period of social difficulty, which was not corrected until Sir Henry's son and heir was made a Baron in the 1690s.

For James Tillie this was therefore a good marriage, and one by which he gained considerable land, including an estate in Durham.

His work and marriage ensured that he quickly became a man of wealth. He was able, when only 35 years old, to buy his knighthood from James I I for the reported sum of £10,000. This is a great sum, twice the estate, for instance, that a rich Lord Mayor of London left his daughter at this time.

Sir James Tillie also had lodgings or offices over the Gate of the Middle Temple. The Middle Temple was a most prestigious place to work, with good court connections, activities, entertainments and the greatest Elizabethan hall in England. It is fair to assume that he must have been an honoured and competent lawyer and his signature witnessed many trust and property deals. He also continued to accumulate wealth himself and to display his status by, for instance, contributing a plate to *Blome's History of the Bible.*

He must have made enemies, and it is thought that it was either they or legal opponents who reported him to The Court of Chivalry for bearing arms to which he was not entitled.

This resulted in a relatively rare court action initiated at the end of 1687on the grounds that he did not have the right to bear the arms '*used in various places in his house and elsewhere'* over the previous three years. They also noted that his arms had angels as supporters, the right to such supporters being restricted only to certain ranks.

In January 1687/8, without having appeared in his own defence, Sir James Tillie was fined £200 with £20 costs.

Some had suggested that he was using a coat of arms from a continental count. This was presumably Johnann Tserclaes, Count of Tilly, known as the most successful general of the thirty years war some fifty years earlier. However, the arms that Sir James adopted were those of a genuine Sir John Tilley (qv) recorded in various heraldic and other documents around the year 1600. These same arms were also found as quarterings in the family of the Earl of Derby, so it is suggested that Sir John Tilley had had no male heir - but that the arms could not pass through his female descendants, if indeed, Sir James Tillie was a descendant. The humiliation of the action in the Court of Chivalry may have been a factor in his leaving London. Another factor may have been his earlier introduction to work for Sir John Coryton and, dare we say it, an admiration for Sir John's wife, Elizabeth.

We do not have the exact date that he started to acquire property in Cornwall, although in papers of the early 1680s, before he was knighted, he was referred to as *James Tillie of Pentillie Castle.*

He began assembling the estate with the house known as Pentearr, which remains marked on the Gascoigne map of 1690. Assembling the estate took him some time, and he continued into old age gaining adjoining land at Bittleford, Tinnel, Hornavers and Halton. It is notable that when he disposed of his many acres of land in different parts of the country it was only the farms immediately around Pentillie that he wished to remain as one inviolate unit.

He was said to have been the steward for Sir John Coryton of Newton Ferrers and to have helped manage the estate on behalf of the young Sir John when he was a child. Gossip and allegation suggested that he had enriched himself at the expense of the Corytons, but no firm evidence survives. The schedule of properties that he owned suggests that he didn't take over any Coryton property.

He appears on Coryton documents from the 1670s including that of the marriage settlement for Elizabeth Chiverton, when he was possibly acting for Elizabeth's father.

He seems to have been the trusted steward of Sir William Coryton between 1690 and 1694, and was also a trustee for family funds and for the Coryton children. Documents show him handling property and funds for the children. Documents attested to his proper handling of the affairs.

Sir James Tillie had accumulated much land, but it does not seem that any had been part of the Coryton Estate. Sir James' lands included much in Plymouth, in Devon, and some estates he purchased in Cornwall. There is no evidence that he stole from the Coryton family. There is, however, evidence that he acted honourably and in their interests.

His connection to the family became closer when, in 1692 and after a decent two year gap, he married Elizabeth, the widow of the late Sir John.

She was a rich lady in her own right, bringing with her land and money granted to her by her father, a former Lord Mayor of London and MP in Cornwall, and for whom a younger Sir James had also acted.

Lady Tillie, by Sir Peter Lely   Sir James Tillie by W Wessing

Although by different artists, the two pictures are within the same cartouche and frames.

The marriage to Elizabeth was in 1692. In that marriage Sir James gained those lands which (with the exception of some bought back by Sir William Coryton), were part of her original dowry.

Perhaps to celebrate his marriage or to honour his new wife he arranged for a London artist to complete a drawing (shown on the next page) for an improved Pentillie Castle. This, like other documents celebrating a marriage, has the intials of the couple in the top corners, with additional shells, cupids and what might be a cheerful man and woman.

Hours have been spent deciphering the initials. The clue seems to be that the lettering is balanced by a duplicate mirror image of the initials. The one on the left is therfore *JT* for James Tillie, that on the right *I* or *L* (for Liz?), *C* for Coryton and a further *C* for her maiden name, Chiverton.

A drawing of the proposal for Pentillie Castle: attrib. Kip and Knyff 1692

Although we have evidence of his work as a lawyer into the 1700s his new wife, Elizabeth, and perhaps retirement from London allowed him to plan the improvements at Pentillie Castle.

There must have been some buildings at Pentillie Castle for twenty years. However, it does not seem that the new work was started until 1698 or 9. These are the dates on three re-used granite doorways placed on the route of what were once entrances to the basement. The doors with pyramid stops and good quality carving have been roughly recut across the lintel and each bears the initals SJT (for *Sir James Tillie*) and the date.

Work continued for some years, and included the laying out of drives, gateways, towers and so on. It may have been interrupted by travels to manage his considerable and far flung estates, and to allow him to continue with legal work.

It would be reasonable to suppose that much of the Castle was complete by 1707, since this is the latest date on the bells for his own chapel tower.

His life remains one of legend and notoriety. Local stories still suggest that he sent out raiding parties to bully neighbours and steal goods, thus requiring the slotted windows in his gate towers. No records confirm this rumour.

Like any other landowner his wine was kept in his own named bottles. This example has a seal for *Sir James Tillie of Pentillie* written around a castle tower. Perhaps the bottle can be taken to attest to his conviviality.

An arrow slot window in the tower by the garden entrance.

A rare bottle with the seal of Sir James Tillie

The lead statue of Sir James Tillie shows him in fine clothes
and carrying a roll of papers 'like a marshall's baton'.

The manner of his burial in 1713, and the mausoleum to which he used to take regular drives to sit and admire the view, contributed to these legends. However, though eccentric, his will is quite sensible, and without the stipulations that later legend suggested. His wishes were carried out after his death, which itself suggests that these wishes were regarded with respect.

Despite his will, Sir James Tillie was a competent, if perhaps sentimental man who had wanted to leave his mark on the world.

Sir James Tillie was certainly ambitious, a self-made man who had done well. He must have been popular with women to have won two such wealthy wives and liked by men to have been succesful in business. He was a man who wanted to rise and indeed did so. He may have had a touch of the 'Del Boy' and been a man who sought advantage, but this was in an age when this was the only way in which business or social life was conducted.

He also seems to have been a somewhat old fashioned man. The designs and architecture of his house and mausoleum confirm that he was a man who looked back to days before the civil war, rather than forward to the changing architecture of the next century.

Sir James Tillie wished to found a dynasty and suggest a lineage more ancient and important than that which he actually possessed, a man who wished to suggest that he was a long established gentleman with lands, castle and family tree.

A statue in unknown material, of Sir James Tillie,
seated in a chair, in the mausoleum, c.1713.

Sir James Tillie: Portrait of Gentleman in wig and blue gown
attrib: Sir Godfrey Kneller c 1690

Much of Sir James' building at Pentillie Castle still remains, despite the alterations that have taken place over the last 300 years. Now smaller than when first built, it is difficult to imagine how unusual were its plan and design.

In 1734 the great house he had built at Pentillie Castle was described:

'This Pentilly is a new name given by himself to this his seat, from its situation on the side of a steep hill, having a pleasant prospect of the country round about. He has adorned it with fine new buildings, composed of several towers with gilded balls and several walks of lime trees on the side of the hill. All which together at a distance made a pretty show'.

The gates by the drive entrance to the garden

Head and shoulders from the lead statue of Sir James Tillie at Pentillie Castle c.1705

The lead statue of Sir James Tillie at Pentillie Castle c.1705,
standing outside his entrance colonnade.

The Tower on Mount Ararat

In 1692 the drawing for Pentillie Castle showed the hill of Ararat as bare. A drawing from 1716 shows it surrounded by fields.

Some have suggested that there may have been some ancient encampment or tower here, but the tower appears to have been entirely the work of Sir James Tillie, who built the platform and provided the ditch to the rear. He called the place Mount Ararat, but suggests it was also known as 'Pisgah'.

Probably built between 1704 and 1712, the square tower has a two storey porch, two upper floors and a crypt or vault, with the principal floor reached by a flight of ten stone steps. It is likely there was once a considerable inscription mounted over the entrance door.

The roof is now missing so it is difficult to see how one got to the higher floor and roof platform. There are also blocked arches and openings whose original design and purpose are not certain.

For many years the entrance was blocked, with a small window through which one could see the statue of Sir James Tillie sitting on his chair and looking over the Tamar. Conflicting stories have arisen about the date of the statue and the

A photograph from the early 19thC.

location of Sir James' body.

The tower and vault were opened by John Tillie Coryton at the beginning of the 19thC. John Tillie Coryton's son Augustus reported that the vault contained the bones of Sir James and that he had been interred in a sitting posture - but within a coffin. He may have been re-buried in St Mellion Church. A 'diviner' has suggested he is in Pillaton churchyard.

The tower has been cleared of undergrowth more than once. The removal of a tree from inside around 1909 brought notoriety and many visitors from Plymouth to the mausoleum. Paths have now been cleared for the walk up to the tower. Through a grill it is possible to make out the life size statue of Sir James Tillie, sitting in a chair and dressed in clothes called old fashioned for the time. The chair has Jacobean strapwork decoration and is itself a fine artefact.

Below the chair was written:

This monument is erected in memory of Sir James Tillie Knt who dyed ye 15th day of Novmbr Anno Dom 1713 and in ye 67th year of his life. Note that his will suggests he was born in 1645, not 1647, as the monument states.

The statue, seen through the grille in 2009, surrounded by ferns

The tower was built for his pleasure during his life, with a first floor room which gave stunning views over the Tamar. It was also intended as his monument. Despite the legends that have accumulated, it is his will that helps tell a simpler story.

This is in two sections, the first having been made in 1704, and the later being further instruction written shortly before he died.

The will is worth quoting in some detail, because it tells so much about the man, his wealth and wishes.

First, it lists much of his property by name, providing evidence of his considerable holdings.

Second, it suggests that the tower was not then built, referring to a monument yet to be erected.

Third, it is good to read lists of goods, particularly the fine coaches and the *Calash* - a light carriage with seats for four.

Fourth, it suggests a man who liked his own way, with penalties for relatives who did not marry as he thought best.

Finally, the will suggests a genuine affection for his men, and implies some respect by them for him. We would like to know why John Cory got a joint of mutton weekly for life.

The following extracts are from the long will written in 1704. It started with the phrase:

'Dei Voluntas Fiat Et mei hac performet'

... *'And I do desire my body may have a private interment at and in such place at Pentillie Castle as I have acquainted my dearest w. the Lady Elizabeth Tillie with and to have such Monument erected and Inscription thereon made as I have desired of my said dearest wife.*

To wife: clothing, jewells, ornaments, books, china, portraits, toys in the closet at Pentillie.
Testator's coach chariot calash and set of 6 horses with choice of 2 other horses and cows. 100 guineas. After wife's death to her grandchildren of Mary and Rich Gotley as she thought fit. In default Albinia Tillie Gotley. Wife to treat nephews kindly.

To Rich. Gotlie, jun. and Mary his w.: for mourning £10 and for her separate use 100 guineas.
To Albinia Tillie Gotley: £500 at day of her marriage with either one of my nephews but if she marries anyone else only to have £250.
To cousin Mary Mattock: £50 on her marriage day. To marry any but Wm. Parkes. (If she does legacy void).

To wife :£50 for funeral 'desiring four of my ancientest Workmen may lay me in my Grave unto whom I give forty shillings each and £10 to Wm. Trenaman.'
To honest Rich. Lawrence in meat and drink for his own person to value of 2s. 6d. per week at Pentillie for life. To domestic servants living with testator at death 40s each. To Samuel Holman, his tools.
To Jn. Cory a joint of mutton weekly for his life.

A photograph taken after the clearance of 1909 gives a good idea of chair, statue and decoration. The material of which the sculpture is made is not known.

In 1713, the year of his death and in his 67th year, he added the following in order to give his followers a clearer idea of his wishes:

'Laying aside the pompous solemnity of a Funeral That by Its Extravagance would devour the Living, following the Methods herein prescribed, I Desire my servant Samuell may within fiftie Houres next after my Death Compose and make for me a Timber oake Chaire, and my Servant John Quilting a Crape or Flannel Lining therefore In which I may sit exactly fit Tight and Close Remaining in One of the little Roomes near Pentillie Library until the Lady Elizabeth Tillie my wife shall order above Fifteen and under Twenty Five of my Men Servants (not Gentlemen Pall-Bearers who make It their Imploy for Lucre not Lovesake) To Carry and lay me in a Repository for that purpose to be made Either on that Eminence called Mount Arraret or Pisgah Giving unto Each of such my Men Servants a Gold Ring and a pair of Gloves'.

These requirements are practical, kind to his men and suggest a wish not to waste money.

We believe that his body remained in the crypt until the early 19thC, but later legend had it that it had been removed to the churchyard. Perhaps renovation of the mausoleum will one day clear up this mystery for us.

The Building of Pentillie Castle:

A Baroque Palace?

Part of the drawing thought to have been prepared in 1692

Sir James Tillie was unusual in planning a house on an entirely new site. So far as we know there had never been a house at the end of this hill overlooking the Tamar. New house sites are rare in Cornwall and indeed, England, because most places with access to water transport and with protection from the weather had already been used. A house of status nearly always replaced or extended an earlier house on the same site.

At Pentillie it is possible that there was an earlier watch tower or building on the headland. It is more likely that the house to which the headland related was that at Pentearr, just east of Pentearr Cross. Pentearr stood at the head of the harbour creek, with shelter from the weather, good water wells and at the centre of the farm's field system.

In 1809 Repton reported that it looked as though the southern tower was of earlier construction, but added that further investigation suggested the whole structure had been built about the same time.

However, Sir James Tillie was described in London documents of the mid 1680s as being *'of Pentillie Castle'*. Either this was a statement of aggrandizement and hope, or he had already pur-

chased Pentearr and started work on a building right on the headland. The southwest corner of the building completed by Sir James does not match the rest of the balanced design. Surviving plans and drawings suggest that this had a hall or dwelling range running east to west, with the great tower on the south east corner. This building, started in the 1680s, appears to have been in an earlier Jacobean style.

It seems that at the end of the 1680s Sir James Tillie spent less time running his lawyer's business from London, and retired or planned to retire to Cornwall. This may have had much to do with the death of one of his clients, Sir John Coryton, and Sir James' marriage two years later to his widow, Elizabeth. It is to this marriage date that we ascribe the 'architect's sketch' for the new building at Pentillie.

In the 1690s the concept of the architect had not yet taken hold. Certainly Wren had designed in accordance with what we would call architectural principle. However, he was 'The King's Surveyor' following classical fashions. Vanbrugh had started life as a stage set designer. Most designs were probably still carried out by a master craftsman according to established traditions, occasional pattern books and the whims of the client.

Because the proposed building shown in the 1692 drawing is so unusual, we should first consider why this is so untypical a scheme and what sort of design Sir James Tillie <u>might</u> have considered.

The first half of the 17thC has been called 'The Great Rebuild', a period when there was relative calm and wealth in the country before the Civil War, and when most houses of status were rebuilt. After the Civil War the influence of the continent, where King and courtiers had been living for fourteen years, changed the view on building, and brought what can be called a new Baroque fashion to architecture. One could also describe it as showy, with some pretensions to classical orders but without, generally, the actual knowledge of continental designs or of the classical architecture which would help order the buildings. This Baroque fashion lasted but a short time, and was also associated with a different sort of house - the villa or multi-roomed residence - different from the sprawling homesteads usual earlier in the century.

Sir James Tillie had his offices in the Temple, and we can assume would have been familiar with the new buildings being erected in London, and the new fashions in country houses.
Houses of the 1680s and 90s were either grandiose or imitated the simple classicism of Inigo Jones, the tastes of Europe and particularly Holland (whence came the reigning monarch).
They may have had gardens laid out but were blocks rather than complex courtyard buildings.

Great houses such as Belton in Lincolnshire, built in an H shape and surrounded by formal gardens and avenues, might have been a fashionable example to follow. Even the Dutch gables of Montacute, built some 80 years earlier, could have been a likely guide.

Royal Citadel Gateway, Plymouth: Designed by Sir Thomas Fitch for Charles II and completed in 1670

Some idea of the originality of Sir James Tillie's design is gained by looking at other houses built around that time in Cornwall, some of which followed the fashions prevalent in the rest of the country. The larger houses include Newton Ferrers, the former house of his new wife.

Stowe, Cornwall. Built 1686
Edmund Prideaux 1716

Newton Ferrers. Built from 1690
Edmund Prideaux 1716

Antony House, built 1721
by Edmund Prideaux 1727

Glynn, near Bodmin: by Edmund Prideaux 1727

Dunsland in Devon rebuilt 1680
by Edmund Prideaux 1716

two storey facade. Bake, near St Germans, had a new house built in front of the old ranges. Menabilly had a new 'classical' wing and facade. More modest houses such as those at Trereife, near Penzance or Rosemerryn in Budock, copied the styles of 1680. Larger houses such as Trewarthenick or Boconnoc were refaced or rebuilt in styles to which Pentillie has little relation.

Two more modest houses are among the earliest of

Tregassow, near Truro, built 1692

Great Treverran, Fowey, built 1704

Antony House was rebuilt a few years later, as was Glynn. Dunsland was built perhaps 20 years before Pentillie Castle.

Both Glynn and Antony have small corner pavilions to the courtyard that reflect the tradition of Montacute. Such features were an important part of the design at Pentillie.

Most new designs of the time had a more classical

their type in the county. Tregassow, built in 1692 by a man also seeking status and the latest fashion, is an astonishing achievement, although old fashioned in interior detail. Treverran of 1704 has wonderful half engaged columns and pretensions to be 'modern', but it is only one room thick with a small right angled service wing. Neither proved an interesting style for Sir James.

Sir James was seeking a castle, a status building which reflected his own sense of importance. I suspect he thought old fashioned tastes better suggested an established family. He did not want to look 'up and coming'.

Ince Castle, probably built of brick around 1640, with patterns, corner towers and a first floor hall, provides some similarity to Pentillie, which had first floor saloons, towers and castellated walls.

The great house at Hardwick Hall, built at the end of the 16thC by a woman who hoped a relative might become queen, has a central entrance colonnade or loggia flanked by two accommodation towers. These loggias seem to have been a short lived fashion in the two decades before the Civil War. Six examples survive in Cornwall.

The north front at Godolphin, Cornwall, had a colonnade and entrance added between two earlier defensive towers. This is similar to the west front of Pentillie, assuming two fewer pillars and differently roofed towers. Godolphin also had an entrance courtyard framed by small towers or pavilions. At Godolphin there were rooms over the entrance and a second colonnade was intended to run round the internal courtyard.

The third picture shows a new house at Hexworthy, where a central two roomed block had a small lower wing to each side.

We can make assumptions about Sir James Tillie's design based on what we know of his life. He was a man from the lower gentry, who had risen high and consorted with the great, but with pretensions, and a perhaps misplaced sense of grandeur. He wished not only 'to make a statement' but also to suggest a long established great house. He may also have been a person of genuinely old fashioned taste. His tomb, for instance, has eared strapwork in a Jacobean design more typical of the period before 1640. Comparison with the monument in

Ince Castle: Drawn by Edmund Prideaux 1727

Godolphin House: The arcaded loggia of 1630 built between two earlier towers.

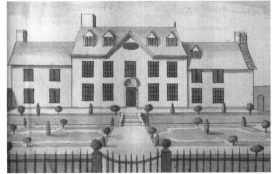

Hexworthy in Cornwall, drawn By Edmund Prideaux 1716

St Mellion of Sir William Coryton emphasises this difference in taste and 'modernity'.

It is interesting that he seems to have re-used second-hand material such as the stone and tudor doorways in the basement and that the finished house was relatively small and only one room deep. Perhaps he valued a building budget.

Finally, he was no doubt affected by the practicalities of the site, the absence of level ground, the wish to impress a new wife and the magnificence of the chosen site.

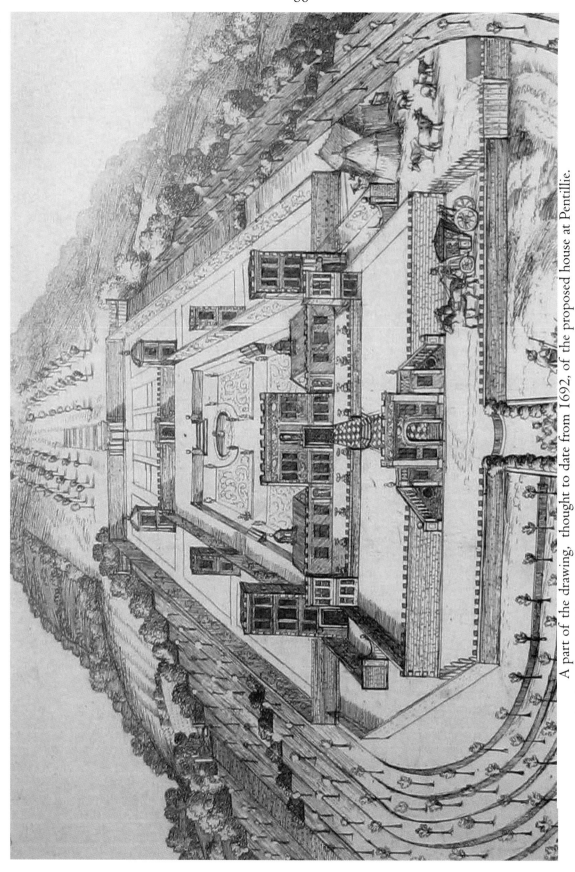

A part of the drawing, thought to date from 1692, of the proposed house at Pentillie.
The drawing should be compared with the conjectural plan of the house as built, on the opposite page.

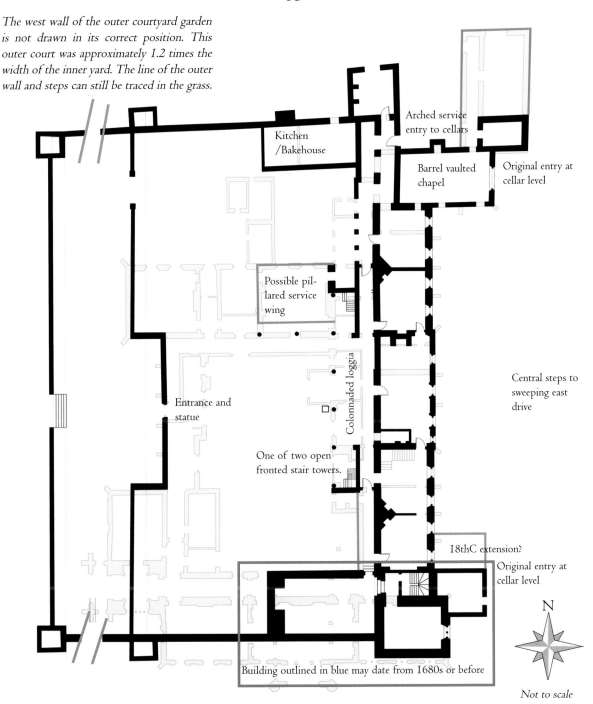

The west wall of the outer courtyard garden is not drawn in its correct position. This outer court was approximately 1.2 times the width of the inner yard. The line of the outer wall and steps can still be traced in the grass.

Arched service entry to cellars

Kitchen /Bakehouse

Barrel vaulted chapel

Original entry at cellar level

Possible pillared service wing

Colonnaded loggia

Central steps to sweeping east drive

Entrance and statue

One of two open fronted stair towers.

18thC extension?

Original entry at cellar level

N

Not to scale

Building outlined in blue may date from 1680s or before

A conjectural plan of Pentillie Castle in 1710

This plan is based on the parts of the building that remain from the 17thC, on examination of the ground, on written evidence and on analysis of the drawings of the house in subsequent centuries.

It must be emphasized that although it fits surviving evidence, this is a conjectural plan. The pillars of the colonnade are marked as blacked points. The ground floors of the two towers are shown open, and with each having a stair to the upper floors. Areas in blue may predate the 1699 build.

Areas outlined in red are thought to be alterations dating from early in the 18thC.

The faded green outline shows the building of 1860 for comparison.

The complete drawing for a new Pentillie Castle, attributed to Kip and Knyff, 1692.

The end of the 17thC saw a fashion for realistic views of houses, first established by Hollar in the 1640s, and continued by Jan Siberects. Jan Kip and Leonard Knyff, both aged about 42 in 1692, introduced a 'bird's eye' approach to representing buildings. They included animals, coaches and horses and illustrated garden plans with some care. They were settled in London and became most famous for producing large books of country house illustration and particularly *Brittannia Illustrata*, printed 1707-9.

Although we do not have their signature on this drawing, it is possible that the proposal for the new house at Pentillie was drawn by them, in London. It was certainly drawn from information rather than a visit because, although quite accurate, it suggests that it was prepared in absentia.

Sadly, the drawing had been cut down at some time to fit a frame and so the edges and, more important, the lower and dedication section are missing. Nevertheless, it seems probable that this drawing was by Kip and Knyff.

Much is accurate in showing the site, with the quarry and the distant hill. Details of interest include the field layout on the way to Mount Ararat, the timber docks, the quarry, the lime kilns and the hint of the inlet to the south.

The design for the house and grounds uses the hill to make a magnificent estate.

It is worth drawing comparisons with the new traditions in France, better known after 1685, when Versailles was more often visited. However, the series of landscaped avenues and long views laid out in this picture are almost certainly the concept of Sir James Tillie himself.

Pentillie from the Tamar(Part). Drawn by Edmund Prideaux in 1717

It is the design of the house and its palatial ambitions that make Pentillie unusual. The floor plan was old fashioned. A central one room deep pavilion stands over a raised basement with a single storey pavilion to each side. This, in the drawing, is separated from the central block by a corridor. Beyond that are flanking work units and towers included to add grandeur. To the west, away from the river, are a sunken garden, walkways and walled enclosures with more perimeter pavilion towers. The picture by Kip and Knyff shows the retention of the cow yard and other service areas, all of which are recognised as important for the house. The main access uses the original road in the valley which was extended to run round the hill and come up a ramp between the house and the river to a grand set of steps before a windowed lodge. This bird's eye view shows a design unlike others of the time. The concept shown in this drawing was unusual in England and can with some justification be called a palace designed around its gardens and approaches, an architectural development not taken further in this form in England. It may be considered unique. It is more astonishing that the house seems to have been built much as shown in the drawing for the proposal.

The provision of a house one room thick with no internal corridor in a pavilion style may have relationship to some of the French hunting lodges and designs of the earlier part of the 17thC, but little relationship to England where the styles of the day looked for regular elevations and houses built with more concessions to comfort and changed social conditions.

We are lucky that we have a couple of drawings from the early 18thC showing the house. The one on this page by Edmund Prideaux dates from around 1717 and the other, shown on page 39, dates from the mid 18thC. Both show an outline which we can relate to the original proposal but which is different in some important aspects.

In 1800 Repton suggests that the tower and buildings at the south end of the slope were much older and that Sir James Tillie had added on to them by extending to the north.

It would be tempting to agree with this, save that Repton himself says that examination of these buildings suggests that they were all built around the same time or, as we believe, in two phases, one starting around 1680 and the other in 1698.

It is also clear that Sir James Tillie landscaped the hill. The original ground level on which the house stands sloped towards the south and east. The basement level was built on the ground and then the ground brought up to suggest that the east entrance was at ground level. The cellar structure, despite the fact that it has a slight bend in it, appears to have been built in one construction. In the cellars are still the windows high in the wall which were intended to be viewed from outside but have been blocked by later terraces. An alternating series of circles and oval windows, these are a 'Baroque edition' based on the Italian fashions of a century earlier. If they could still be viewed, the principal floor would stand slightly above the ground, giving it more importance. It might even have required steps up to the entrance on the inner or courtyard side.

We should not overlook that parts of the facade to west and east elevations were built in brick, a material and colour rare in Cornwall at this time.

Alteration in 1968 re-established the columned arcade, the courtyard of the main block, and the two flanking towers which once had pepperpot roofs, described in the 18thC as old fashioned or Elizabethan.

Sir James Tillie's Pentillie

It is thought that the entire site, gardens and landscape were the creation of Sir James Tillie. They remain one of the earliest surviving great landscapes in Cornwall.

It was a difficult site with steep hills and valleys. Nevertheless the avenues were laid out and a large number of buildings erected. These included gateways, a wall across the width of the headland, and towers. Legend suggests he was so unpopular with his neighbours that he had to defend himself from ruffian attack. This seems most unlikely. It is more likely that they are part of a romantic landscape, more garden ornament than defence. A first tower still stands by the garden entrance, although it is possible that this is south of Sir James Tillie's original avenue gateway.

One of the original curved gate piers still in postion on the east, before the original short drive to the coach yard.

An arbour with plenty of lamp niches, built on the west boundary at the end of one of his avenues.

The outermost tower, north of the gates with arrow slits and later window openings.

Remnants of a second tower stand just down the drive. Repton refers to another one, whose site cannot be clearly identified. It seems possible, therefore, that Sir James Tillie had planned to have a series of towers which would be passed on the way to his house. Once at the house of 1700, you would be faced by a large blank castellated wall enclosing the courtyards. The central door leads through to the second yard in which stands the statue of the man himself and beyond him, the colonnade of five and two half columns (of Elizabethan rather than classical design). Another column lies in pieces, so we may assume that the colonnade ran down two wings, the one to the south perhaps for owners' apartments, and that to the north for service. Although Henry VIII had installed internal corridors at Hampton Court in the 1540s, Pentillie was designed without them. One room led through to another unless one went outside to the colonnaded but covered loggia.

The deep loggia formed the long entrance porch to the main hall or saloon. This was heated by a large fireplace at one end and had windows looking over the river. To each side was a pair of saloons, each heated by an angled chimney stack. The east windows may have been large, divided by transoms and mullions, as in the Knyff drawing. Above the entrance loggia an undivided 'long gallery' with three narrow windows ran between the towers, looking over the court. Parts of the entrance used expensive, fashionable brick with a moulded string course. In addition to a south wing a north wing may have enclosed the courtyard. Further north were service buildings round a second court, with the bakehouse or kitchen. Further to the north still were yards, gardens including fruit walls, melon gardens, a cow house, farm yard, barn, coach house and stables. Walls and pavilions separated the owner's area from the animals, services and supply routes to the basement.

The floor of the main *salon*, the present dining room, has a typical 17thC construction of wide timbers. Note some have been reused.

Below is a section of studding which suggests the pattern of Jacobean panelling, which may have lined the walls of the house.

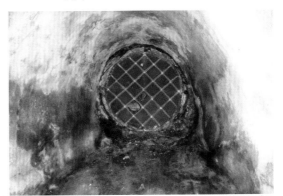

High in the basement walls is a series of small windows, alternating circles and ovals, with one rectangular one. This one, although blocked to the outside, retains its original glass.

Below is a piece of carved timber, found re-used. This suggests that the original decorative scheme would have had much such carved timber. We can only guess that the house must have had fine woodwork and heavy Jacobean stair cases.

Two ceilings remain at the north of the main house, which are of typical 1690 design.

To the north east was formerly a chapel on two floors. The original barrel-vaulted ceiling structure remains.

This vaulted and square pavilion with a fireplace on the first floor might have been an estate office. To the left is the original entrance to the lower or basement service floor.

This picture shows the rear of the original service block, with a further entrance to the basement, and the remnants of the massive bakehouse or kitchen chimney. One of the original pavilions remains, cut short to the right.

This aerial view gives a good idea of how the courtyard might have existed, if the 1968 pavilions can be imagined replaced by wings to the courtyard. Off to the left was a lower section of service yards and kitchen gardens.

This east view of the clock tower shows a blocked Gothic window or entry to the old stable yard. To the left is the altered gable end of the chapel, also with a blocked entry to the service basement.

The clock tower must have been a prize possession. The workings, B, for the clock, still tell the time. The bell on the tower proudly bears the inscription: *Sir James Tillie 1707*. So also does each of the set of six bells, C & D, dated variously 1705 to 1707. They are said to have been re-hung and rung for the marriage of William and Evelyn in 1887.

Pentillie Castle during the 18th Century

Pentillie from the Tamar: Drawn by Edmund Prideaux in 1717

We are not certain how much of the house was finished, when Sir James Tillie died in 1713. We can assume that it was fine enough for his wife to continue living there. The difficulty is that the interior and much of the appearance is now of the 18th century, rather than the heavier Jacobean or Baroque interiors which we judge were preferred by Sir James.

The exterior of the house is shown in this drawing by Edmund Prideaux and in a picture from 1813.

Pentillie on the Tamar:
Drawn by J Farrington Esq; Engraved by J Landseer ARA & Published May 3 1813 by T Cadell & W Davies, Strand

Pentillie on the Tamar: artist, printer & date unkown: thought to be mid 18thC.

Pentillie from the Tamar: oil painting by William Payne c 1790

At the end of the 18thC, the house retains the great southern tower, with the pavilions to the north and beyond them the chapel extension and the smaller bell tower. The quay on the river continues to be of importance with lime kilns, quarry warehouses and other buildings.

It is also clear from the family history that, save in the early decades of the 18thC, the family spent years in legal difficulties and it is unlikely that any money was spent on the house. It is also said that the last 30 years of the century was a period of neglect, with so little maintenance that the house was left in a poor state.

We assume that any changes were carried out in the first half of the 17thC, perhaps when James (Wooley) Tillie was made Sheriff in 1734.

It is possible that the shields added to the well house and lime kiln by the river, and which show the Tillie arms granted in 1733, suggest the date of the works. The date of 1668 cut into the one by the lime kiln is puzzling. Perhaps an old stone was reused and the shield recut?

In order to follow the changes carried out in the 18thC it may be easier to refer to the conjectural plan for the first building on page 31.

The 18thC staircase photographed in 2009

We can take a stab at what these changes involved. First, it is possible that the southern of the three pavilions envisaged by Sir James had not been finished. The 1717 drawing appears to show that an older gable end range still stood. This is not certain, since the present 18thC stair shown in the picture above, appears to have been fitted in an earlier building.

Second, the stairs were removed from the towers at each end of the colonnade, and the new stair hall (shown in the photograph above), achieved by dividing one of the salons in two.

Third, a further extension was added to the north of that which already lay east of the southern tower. This earlier extension, south-east of the other ranges, perhaps balanced the chapel at the northern end, or formed part of an earlier building.

The windswept original design was improved by further works within the colonnade and by the addition of a service wing at the north west end of the colonnade, where was sited a kitchen more convenient to the house. The corridor through the colonnade was extended to the south, resulting in the blocking of the cellar windows to the west. This allowed sheltered passage to the south wing.

The draughts of the original design were reduced by division of the colonnade.

The cellar windows being already blocked to the west, it is probable that changes were made to the outside levels, to allow easier access to what had been the front door to the east. This resulted in the blocking of the remaining variegated Baroque cellar windows to the east and of the cellar entrances originally provided by Sir James Tillie to the east.

The arcade to the service rooms and to the chapel on the extreme north remained.

A further service building was built against the north-east bell tower.

Throughout the century the house remained one room thick. Upstairs there were steps between the central and side blocks, and the rooms led off each other.

Downstairs, the house was remodelled. The ceilings to the two salons at the north end retain designs typical of the 1690s and are probably part of the original build. A new interior scheme used pilasters and a modillion cornice. The cornice and decorative detail with fully engaged reeded pilasters and complex capitals do not appear to form part of the more organised later classical tradition. There was still no corridor between the rooms of

The lower stair hall, looking south, photographed in 2009.
The repositioned door case has both 'Greek key' and 'shouldered' features.

the main range. However, there were cupboards, alcoves and pilasters whose detail appears to have survived.

One puzzling detail is the Greek key design that appears on some mouldings around the stair. These could be 18thC, could be typical of 1810, but may be part of the earliest scheme.

Another puzzle is the 'eared' door at the bottom of the stairs, a remnant perhaps of the original design, and which may therefore have been reused from elsewhere.

It seemed that the double angled fireplaces to each of the side *salons* might have been later insertions. It is now believed they were part of the original and unusual design. The fireplaces were, however, improved and altered during the 18thC. The fire place in the stair hall, shown in the photograph to the right, is a particularly fine work of reeded marble. The carved wood surround has dentils and

eagles with fruit. The surround may indeed be older than the insert, which is similar to those found at Antony House and at Boconnoc, where in both cases they date from about the third decade of the 18thC. This is an exceptionally fine fireplace.

During the 18thC, panelling appears to have been renewed, although there are signs under existing partitions that Sir James Tillie's heavier and differently proportioned panelling may have survived in some places. This suggests that all his rooms were so panelled.

Another alteration included the division of the main central *salon*, by the addition of a partition to form a service lobby at the north end. This blocked the original large fireplace, and resulted in a further fireplace being added to the south end of that room.

The picture to the left shows the reeded pilasters, complex capitals, and eared door (now in a cupboard) that once opened from the main salon to the room to the north. The picture on the right shows details of the 18thC scheme of decoration.

It also seems possible that changes were made in two areas of Sir James Tillie's original design.

First, it is likely that the windows were changed in aspect and perhaps in size from the original transom and mullioned casement windows. We have no record of either their original design or their 18thC form.

A second puzzle is the extent of the 1700 house, and whether that included a wing projecting north of the main west courtyard. It is probable that the 18thC saw either the building of such a wing or its alteration.

Two watercolours by Humphrey Repton, drawn in 1809/10 for his 'Red Book'
and showing the west and east elevations before the alterations of 1812.

Two drawings and a plan prepared by Repton show the appearance and details of part of the floor plans for the house in 1809 before any of the alterations of 1812.

The first watercolour shows Pentillie Castle from the west with its two 'Elizabethan' towers, perhaps in red brick, and the castellated wall to the courtyards.

The second shows the house from the river. The small brick wings at each end of the main facade are clearly shown. The steps in the centre of the eastern terrace suggest that the basement windows and entrances are already lost. The sloping wall with arch supports (which still survives today) marks the line of Sir James Tillie's great east entrance drive to gateway and stable yard.

The Heraldry of Pentillie

Heraldry describes the terms and way in which emblems identified those entitled to bear a 'coat of arms'. It was said to have started as a way of recognizing friends or foes in battle, but the bearing of arms quickly became a matter of social status, and of pride. Inspectors made regular tours in an attempt to record and control the grant and use of arms, and the College of Arms, with its advisors or policemen called Heralds, still exists. The last such inspection for Cornwall took place in 1620.

Coats of Arms became the important definition of social status and position. Indeed, it became important to show that you were descended from the 'right people' in as many generations and from as many armigerous ancestors as possible.

As a result, arms became quartered or divided with the addition, according to strict rules, of the arms of each different strand of one's ancestors. These 'quarterings' were not only a matter of pride, but also of complexity.

Much of the art of Heraldry is overlooked nowadays, but remains a useful tool in trying to identify building owners, phases and the occupiers of church tombs. The colourful designs and complex imagery is fascinating. Pentillie Castle retains many survivals.

Sir James Tillie

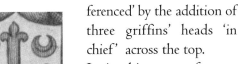

The first picture, on the right, shows the arms claimed by the first Sir John Tillie, the use of which resulted in his being taken to court.

"Argent, a cross Flory, between four crescents gules". To you and me this means a red cross with flowery ends, with four red crescents in the corners on a silver background. Above the coat of arms was probably the crest of a phoenix rising from flames. To each side of the shield was an angel acting as a 'supporter'.

The second example, top right, shows the grant of arms recorded in 1733 to the Tillie family. This was based on those claimed by Sir James Tillie, but 'differenced' by the addition of three griffins' heads 'in chief' across the top.

It is this coat of arms which can be found added above the granite door to the lime kiln down by the river, shown in the picture below. It also has some Jacobean decoration, but the date of 1657, which is long before the grant in 1733, is a puzzle. Was the lintel recut? The same blazon is above the finely cut door to the well, also by the river.

Coryton Heraldry

St Mellion church has brightly coloured, although rather worn, examples of Coryton quarterings on the splendid memorial of Sir William (died 1651) and his wife and the equally wonderful memorial to a later Sir William (died 1711) and his wife.

In 1813, proud of the family blazon and the number of quarterings achieved, John Tillie Coryton retained the Windsor Herald to record his family's descent and their coats of arms.

The arms of John Tillie Coryton, showing the six 'quarterings' of his descent.

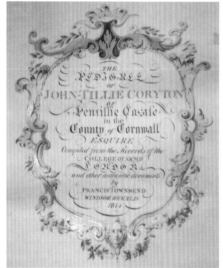

The dedication from the family tree presented to John Tillie Coryton by the Windsor Herald, in 1813.

This showed the entitlement to a satisfactory number of quarterings and descent from lots of the 'right' people.

The most important of the arms, the 'main line', is that in the top left hand corner, where the black Coryton saltire cross is shown.

Set on the walls of Pentillie can still be seen the uncoloured carved shields of John Tillie Coryton, who rebuilt the house in 1810.

These arms date from after his marriage.

They are the same as those in the hatchment for his wife shown on the following page. They combine the Coryton/Tillie arms to the left and the arms of Leveson Gower, his wife, to the right.

The arms of John Tillie Coryton, to the left with the arms of his wife, Elizabeth Leveson Gower, to the right.

In practice, the crest formed a more practical method of identification. The Coryton crest is a lion with the motto *'Dum spiro spero'*- while I breathe I hope.

The first picture to the right, on this page, shows the large diamond shaped painting which hangs in the hall of Pentillie Castle. This painting was almost certainly a 'hatchment', a word derived from 'achievement', meaning coat of arms. 'Hatchments' were hung in churches for a year to commemorate the death of the person whose arms are described. Nowadays the name behind the coat of arms is often unknown. This hatchment probably commemorates the death of John Tillie Coryton's wife, Elizabeth, in 1824. The diamond shows that it is a woman. The right hand side has Elizabeth's arms, those of the Leveson Gower family.

The motto is not that of any family, but rather the phrase *'In coelo quies'* or 'rest in heaven'.

The second picture to the right shows the simplified arms of the Coryton family. This has the saltire differenced by a horseshoe and the blue tongued lion crest, which should also have a horse-shoe.

The heraldic description for the Coryton blazon is now: *'Argent, a saltire sable charged on the fesse point with a horseshoe or'.* The description of the crest is *'A lion passant gules, charged on the shoulder with a horse-shoe as the arms'.*

Finding date stones and coats of arms can lead to dead ends. The third picture on this page shows a beautifully cut slate sun dial, now re-hung on the 1968 south portico. It tells the 'correct' time, although this could be debated since Cornish time is apparently half an hour different fron that of London.

The blazon has a chevron with three balls, which may be the arms of the Bond family who were from Erth, opposite Antony House. The little crescent hanging above the chevron is the mark for a second son.   I suspect that this sun dial has been re-sited from elsewhere and that it is nothing to do with the Tillie or Coryton family.

The sun dial is engraved with the phrase *Quotidie Morior,* and the date 1693.

The Gardens at Pentillie Castle

There are over 50 acres of garden at Pentillie, and round them a further 200 acres of landscaped parkland intended to create views, drives and walks, extensive and beautiful woodlands and a setting for the house.

Many places have large gardens, but few can claim to have been first laid out around 1700, with designs, curiosities, avenues and spectacular effect. Sir James Tillie deserves some fame for his designs on what was then a green field site. He also provided a series of walled gardens such as 'the melon ground', a long south facing wall for the growing of fruit, vegetable gardens, and so on. His landscape features included stone arbours and other curios.

Most owners have been devoted to the gardens and grounds. At the end of the 18thC the gardens were already recognised as special. Visitors made much

The plan below is intended to give some idea of the scale of the gardens and the extent of the different phases of work. Areas coloured or outlined in red show areas and drives laid out by Sir James Tillie. Blue outlines the changes arising from the work of Repton, Kennedy and Mrs Elizabeth Coryton after 1809. A further phase outlined in green covers the works added by Augustus and his sister Charlotte Coryton, between 1855 and 1890.

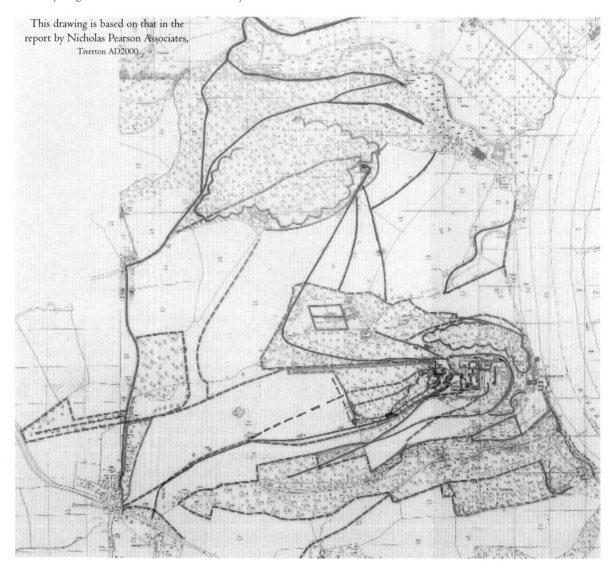

This drawing is based on that in the report by Nicholas Pearson Associates, Tiverton AD2000.

The Lime Walk entrance with posts recovered from Clifton Manor. Below is a mid 19thC ornamental pot.

The lime avenue, cobbled and planted in 1861 by Michael Parker for the sum of £36.9s.11 1/2d

of the 'rich and noble woods' the fine situation and 'beautiful woods which overspread the rising hills are surrounded...by the circumfluent waters and in every point of view appear the most picturesque beauty'. (John Swete)

Others commented on the 'luxuriant' views.

It is suggested that the family had been interested in the gardens during the 18thC because they were based at Pentillie rather than absentee owners with a life in London. However, it is said there had been much decay during the last decades of the century, perhaps confirmed by the reports of luxuriant growth.

Much was achieved, but took some time to mature, because in 1820 it was noted that 'The remains of the gardens and shrubberies show them to have been very extensive...'

A new energetic owner, with a wife most interested in gardening, asked the famous Humphrey Repton to make proposals. These were extended by Lewis Kennedy, also famous for his garden designs. Gardens were important to Elizabeth, John Tillie Coryton's wife, who was renowned for her interest in the garden.

The garden was listed as one of the most important of Cornish gardens in JC Loudon's encyclopaedia of 1822.

By the middle of the 19thC a great garden was well established. New kitchen gardens had been built and the 1850s saw work on the glass houses and houses and areas for specialist produce. The drives were extended, and more seats and curiosities provided.

By now the head gardener had become a person of importance. In 1842 it was said that the head gardener of the time, then 80 years old, had worked there 50 years. There were also comments on the absence of weeds on the paths and drives, achieved by the application of debris from lead and copper mines, poisonous to plants and possibly, we would now suggest, not good for humans. It is said that three successive head gardeners had each achieved many decades service in the century to the end of the First World War.

From the 1850s Colonel Augustus Coryton and his sister Charlotte oversaw an increase in pace and labour with the operation of a grand garden. They bought and grew seed, imported manure and car-

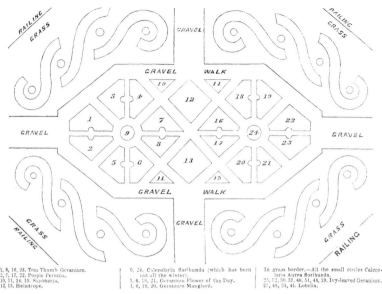

1, 8, 16, 23. Tom Thumb Geranium.
2, 7, 17, 22. Purple Petunia.
10, 11, 14, 19. Saponaria.
12, 13. Heliotrope.

9, 24. Calceolaria floribunda (which has been out all the winter).
5, 4, 18, 21. Geranium Flower of the Day.
3, 6, 19, 20. Geranium Manglesii.

In grass border.—All the small circles Calceolaria Aurea floribunda.
25, 52, 30, 37, 46, 51, 44, 59. Ivy-leaved Geranium.
27, 48, 24, 41. Lobelia.

A plan for one of the flower gardens at Pentillie Castle, illustrated in *The Journal of Horticulture*, 1863, vol II

ried out all phases of garden operations. Gardening became a 'substantial' activity. The first cast iron boiler had been provided in 1826, but new boilers were provided to heat fruit and glass houses. Records show that flowering plants or shrubs were shipped in from Belgium, and increasingly there was potting, growth from seeds and cuttings and purchases from many nurseries. This phase has described the gardens as being a 'plantsman's garden'. Plans for one of the formal flower gardens show complex geometric patterns and 24 different flowering beds, with decorative hedges, lawns and so on. Ledgers record many years with foreign plant purchases.

William & Evelyn Coryton continued a garden tradition with no particular changes, save for the importation around 1904 of a great number of specialist plants from America, giving rise to the creation of the American Garden, still in place today and which then included *Kalmias, Andromedaas, Rhododendrons, Ghent and Evergreen Azaleas and Benthamidia Fragifera,* in various beds.

Most of the terraces to the south and east were realigned during the 19thC, with new steps and paths, which overlaid the original scheme and walks of Sir James Tillie. The end of the Victorian period also saw rebuilt gar-

deners' cottages, service buildings and a new sawmill.

The gardens included at this time two quarry gardens, several summer houses or curiosity buildings, including the thornery, the root house and a house built of knuckle bones. There were many gateways, avenues, wells, roofed seats, alcoves, a boat house, decorative bridges and so on. Despite the acres of garden it was the scenic beauty that attracted comment. Many visitors started to come, sometimes by steamer, to admire the gardens from the end of the 19thC onwards.

One commentator said

Coming round the land and catching the house suddenly from the water, the effect is much heightened, The stranger unconsciously 'suspends the dashing oar' that he may enjoy to the fullest extent a scene so charmingly picturesque.

From the end of the First World War, the gardens necessarily decayed, with fewer staff, lesser funding and also uncertainty about the future.

The gardens are now being cleared and plans prepared for restoration. They are still full of wonderful plants, but also of delights that remain to be explored, hinting at many discoveries yet to come.

Humphrey Repton 1752-1818

Humphrey Repton has been called the 'last great English landscape designer of the 18th Century'. Although seen as a successor to Capability Brown, he was more modest in outlook than his predecessors and believed in the importance of vistas to give scale and sight lines to a landscape. He emphasised the importance of lodges and features and would use surrounding country, even villages, to provide longer vistas, and increase the apparent scope of an owner's landscape.

Repton also saw himself as a specialist consultant, rather than designer and contractor, and felt able to give advice not just on landscape and the positioning of buildings, but on the architecture of buildings themselves. Repton, who created his career rather than being trained for it, was famous because he prepared for most of his clients a 'red book', that is, a book with many pictures showing what he proposed for his 'picturesque' landscapes of great houses. These red books, called after their binding, gave explanatory text and watercolours with overlays, which showed houses both before and after his proposed alterations. The red book for Pentillie Castle was drafted during a visit 'on the spot' in September 1809 and the book prepared in Essex and dated February 1810. Much of the work may have been carried out by his deaf elder son John Adey Repton, since Repton himself was not well at the time and was feeling his age.

His books on garden design were amongst the earliest of this type of publication for Britain and the three publications of 1795, 1803 and 1816 contribute to his reputation and the respect in which his work is now held. Despite the fact that so many of his suggestions were eventually rejected

Repton was generally tactful. Although capable of being fairly spiteful about some of his contemporaries, he always flattered the client.

Humphrey Repton had prepared a number of schemes in Cornwall. These had included Port Eliot in 1792, Trewathenick in 1793, Antony in 1794 Catchfrench in 1794 and Tregothnan in 1809 for a cousin of Mrs Coryton. Repton was recommended to Pentillie by Sir Reginald Pole Carew who had been enthusiastic with Repton's ideas for Antony. For his part, Repton was recommended to visit Pentillie since work there would gain *'The admiration of all who explore the banks of the Tamar...you will therefore have the Eyes of all upon you in what you do'*.

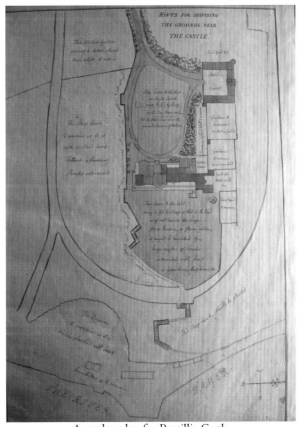

A garden plan for Pentillie Castle
from Repton's 'Red Book' of 1810

Repton's proposal for the west front of Pentillie Castle in 1810

The 'Red Book' for Pentillie is marvellous, finely bound with his scripted comments, with flattery, and his trademark lifting tabs to display the value of proposed schemes. These are particularly useful to us because they help give some idea of the house before the alterations of 1810. They have been shown on earlier pages. Much of his proposal was good, indeed his suggestions for the house seem better than those eventually achieved.

He recommended walks, sheep mown lawns, vistas, and curious buildings, including one made entirely of old roots. He also urged further 'Rosaries' or flower gardens and large masses of shrubs, intermixed with fruit.

Much of what he suggested was carried out by the Corytons, but not by Repton or his sons, perhaps because of his ill health. William Wilkins, the architect chosen for the work, had worked with Repton's son. Repton's work had a greater influence than he had perhaps thought, and can be seen throughout the gardens.

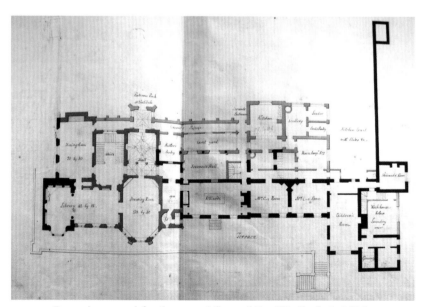

Repton's proposal for the ground floor of Pentillie Castle in 1810

Lewis Kennedy 1752-1818

The introductory page of Lewis Kennedy's 'Green Book' of 1813

Lewis Kennedy was from a family of garden designers who had long held nurseries in Hammersmith, London. Indeed Lewis Kennedy was the fourth generation in this trade and he had a fine reputation for garden advice and design. Associated with gardeners, with architects and many owners of great houses, he completed work on famous gardens in Scotland (notably at Drummond Castle. Other gardens included Dunkeld, Stow in Norfolk, Oddington, Chiswick House, Trent Park and Buckhurst Park. In France he worked for the Empress Josephine at Malmaison and is said to have been taken prisoner during the Napoleonic wars while doing so.

In 1813 Lewis Kennedy was asked to give his own proposals for the gardens at Pentillie Castle. He provided plans and sketches, of which examples are shown here. He acknowledged that his ideas were a development of Repton's.

There is in his suggestions a hint of the fashionable without real originality. He has a thatched root house, a romantic quarry, a rockery, a swiss bridge, a winding dell, a thorn wood and a variety of 'partial landcapes'. He hoped for more rose, jasmine, honeysuckle, shrubs and alpines. He also suggested a flower garden with trellis seats and for the many children of Elizabeth Coryton, a children's garden with a plot for each, rustic arcades and seats.

The terraces also received attention.

He wrote at length with his ideas, and discussed them with Mrs Coryton, with whom he must have got on well. Many of his suggestions were implemented.

The illustrations are taken from his beautifully presented and bound report, known as 'The Green Book'.

An illustration from Lewis Kennedy's 'Green Book' of 1813 for the 'thornery' and 'root house', with a walled garden in the background.

The plan by Lewis Kennedy from his 'Green Book' of 1813, shows a scheme for the gardens west of the house. North is to the right.

John Tillie Coryton 1773-1843
and a Regency Rebuilding.

John Tillie Coryton was living at Crocadon when his father, John Coryton, died in 1803. Aged 30, this was also the year of his marriage to Elizabeth Leveson Gower. One source suggests that his relations continued to live at Pentillie, while he and his wife were at Crocadon, and that therefore it was not until 1809 that John Tillie Coryton could plan for the future of Pentillie Castle.

It is said that the house was in a poor state. Repton commented on how the main room had entrances on both sides, and was always cold. The house needed updating, and also needed to meet the grander pretensions of a wealthy landowner with, so it is said, over 20,000 acres.

It is interesting that the Corytons chose to remain in Cornwall, despite owning property in Devon and elsewhere. It is notable that while other families chose to seek power and influence in London, the Corytons appear to have been happy living in and running their estates in Cornwall. This was unusual for county gentry of this wealth and influence.

Repton had prepared plans for the gardens and good designs for the house. They appear practical and better looking - but not so grand as the eventual plans approved.

Perhaps because Repton himself was not well and not chasing work so far from London, William Wilkins was chosen to make Pentillie a 'modern' Gothic castle. Repton's son was working with William Wilkins so it is assumed this was the source of the introduction.

Elizabeth Leveson Gower, who had married John in 1803, had seven sons and five daughters, of whom nine survived infancy.

John Tillie Coryton saw himself as a man of importance and status, retaining a herald to prove his aristocratic descent. He not only rebuilt the house as a more impressive Gothic castle but further developed and extended the gardens.

John Tillie Coryton

Elizabeth Leveson Gower as a young girl

Elizabeth Leveson Gower circa 1803

William Wilkins 1778-1839

William Wilkins was the son of a builder/architect, also called William, who had carried out work for Repton. As a young man, William had studied at Cambridge, and toured Greece and Italy. His early commissions reflected his affection for Greek classical styles.

He was responsible for much work for universities and public bodies. He designed Downing College in Cambridge, University College in London, St George's Hospital, Hyde Park, and The National Gallery in London, which last was completed in 1838.

His country houses are less well known, perhaps because most were in the 'Tudor Gothic' style, which was popular with his clients.

In this style he completed the front court of King's College, Cambridge. Other college work included new courts for Trinity and Corpus Christi, which last was his own favourite.

In 1809 he had used the Greek revival style for a country house at Grange Park, Hampshire, but most of his country house designs seem to have been in Tudor Gothic, including the remodelling of the great house at Tregothnan, near Falmouth. He has been praised for 'charm and inventiveness' but also criticised for being incompetent at presenting the bulk of a building and its extensions, prissy in detail and weak in mass. However, he was and is admired for much of his work. The volume of work which still stands is considerable.

It was therefore to William Wilkins, recommended by Repton, that John Tillie Coryton turned, around 1810, for plans to modernise and extend Pentillie Castle. Building started in 1812.

The original plans have not been found, but drawings of the elevations he proposed are shown here.

Repton's ideas for alteration had added the great rooms, without the extensions suggested by Wilkins.

The new house was built around the old courtyard. The existing buildings had Gothic buttresses added and the old courtyard was enclosed by buildings. Three new grand rooms for entertainment were added to the south.

One of the difficulties of the old building had been the entrance, which had been either along the valley to gain the east side, with a good climb up the steps, or through the courtyards to the west.

Now, the building had a new projecting porch and obvious entrance standing out towards the main drive. A further Gothic porch was added to the south side.

The old buildings and the old courtyard, relegated to service, and increasingly cluttered through the years by small additions, became unimportant. The statue of Sir James Tillie was relegated to a position alongside a service pantry, standing against a wall, unseen.

William Wilkins' design for the west front, circa 1810

William Wilkins' design for the south front circa 1810

William Wilkins' design for the east front circa 1810

The design had the merit of using the foundations and something of the previous work, but it included blocking in the pillared arcade of Sir James Tillie. Corridors and some internal reorganisation made the house more acceptable to the taste of the time.

The work of John Tillie Coryton in the gardens cannot be overlooked. His wife in particular was noted at the time as devoted to her garden.

The house must have been alive with the large family of Coryton children, with many staff and servants, and many gardeners.

Pentillie Castle had become a great country house, with a large garden, backed by an impressive estate.

The family crest, here shown applied to the hopper heads, was borne with pride.

This page shows some prints done circa 1820 for John Tillie Coryton, to celebrate his re-building.

Pentillie Castle:
A view from the west by Allom, showing the owner watching a gardener before going off shooting, with his dogs.

Pentillie Castle on the Tamar:
drawn by W Westall; engraved by E Francis.
This drawing emphasises the buttresses supporting the made up ground to the south.

This drawing is titled:

To John Tillie Coryton Esq. This south west view of Pentillie Castle in the County of Cornwall, engraved at his expence as an encouragement to this work, is most respectfully inscribed by his obedient servant C S Gilbert.

The coloured coat of arms is that of John Tillie Coryton.
The print was engraved by J C Stadler, and dates from around 1816.

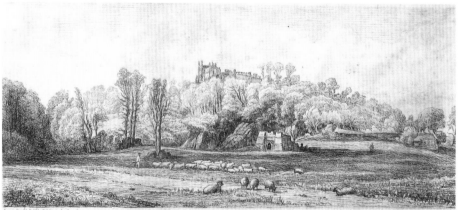

Pentillie Castle, engraved by FC Lewis during the time of John Tillie Coryton:
This shows that the towered entrance to the lime kilns had been completed.

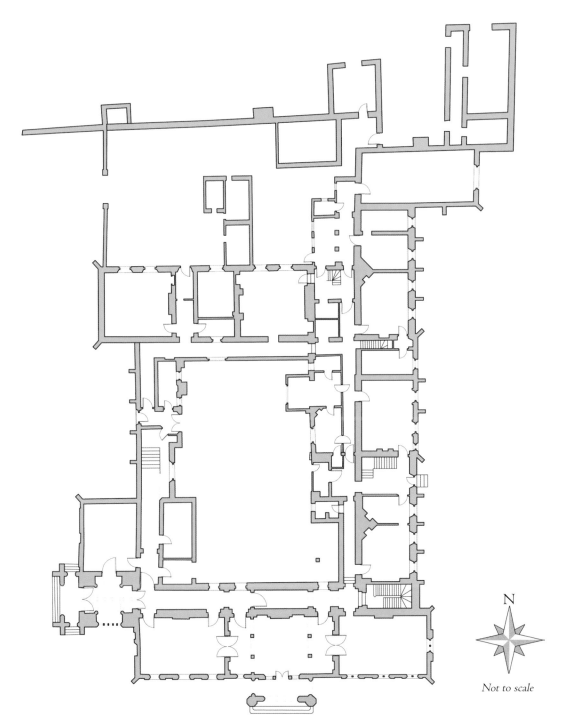

N

Not to scale

A plan of Pentillie Castle prepared in 1867

This plan is based on those drawn up by William Wilkins, and shows the ground floor plan in 1867 before proposals for alteration. The alterations were never carried out although they included a grand double stair hall just north of the south wing. The alterations that were made were minor, such as adding service areas, or altering window layouts. One revealing change was the completion of a corridor for the west side of the first floor of the east range, suggesting that rooms had, until then, continued to open off each other.

Colonel Augustus Coryton 1809-1891
Stability with a Beneficent Squire

John Tillie Coryton died in 1843. His heir had been the eldest son, William, until William died in 1836 at the age of 28, leaving a daughter but no heir. Therefore, Augustus, the second son, inherited at the age of 34.

Colonel Augustus never married, but the house remained the base for the extensive families of his brothers and sisters and their many relatives. His sister Charlotte also never married and lived with him at Pentillie, surviving Augustus by a few years. Augustus had been a Captain in a line regiment. On leaving the army he joined the militia, where he became Colonel of the Cornwall Rangers, using the title most of his life.

Augustus may have contemplated matrimony, since either marriage or the promise of a great position could have been behind the plans to aggrandize the house in the 1860s. The proposals included a staircase that would have been suitable for a Hollywood set. It never happened, the proposals were abandoned, and the money saved.

Although his sister Charlotte lived with him, Augustus enjoyed a bachelor existence. It is said he had a reputation as a convivial character although it is also recalled that there was never any conviviality on a Sunday, a day always taken seriously.

It is possible that the beautifully made cane walking stick, which has a hollow interior and a carefully made silver cap and cup, was his. This provided a variation on the more normal hip flask and meant that on a walk with this stick, refreshment was never far away.

Colonel Coryton never seems to have considered becoming an MP, taking an interest in county or central government politics, or staying in London for the sake of influence or money. He took part in Militia events and training. He was a magistrate and served as High Sheriff of Cornwall in 1848, but remained based at Pentillie where he took his duties as a great landowner seriously.

His obituary in *The Western Morning News* referred to the fact that he had held in hand some 1,500 acres, and that when a farm became free he took it over and improved it before it was relet.

He had the administration of some 20,000 acres in Cornwall and some lands remaining to the family in Devon. He must have got on well with his agent because the same man served as his agent for 40 years.

A cane walking stick with lined interior flask and silver cap or cup

He took an interest in farming, and saw himself as a benign landlord. Although insistent on good farming practice, he could be lenient over rents in times of trouble.

Augustus purchased Halton Quay, to the north of Pentillie, and also rebuilt Pentillie Quay with granite in 1855. He oversaw the 'prettying' of the lime kilns and rebuilding of cottages down by the river. Timber appears to have been another successful and growing business. Saw mills and timber yards were developed; shipments of timber and of bark took place from the quays. The gardens continued to be improved, and though it is now difficult to differentiate exactly which parts can be attributed to Augustus rather than to his father, it is clear that he had inherited an enthusiasm for gardening from both father and mother. Although the vegetable gardens had been moved from their old position before 1841 and new enclosures built, these gardens were extended and gardeners' cottages added.

A new Lime Walk with cobbled road was laid and planted in 1861 (at a cost of just over £36). This lime walk is entered through gates which include a re-used date stone. This probably reflects his purchase of the old mansion of Clifton, which was demolished and where a new house was then built. He and Charlotte took a paternal interest in the affairs of the farmers, tenantry and villagers. They helped build or enlarge village schools and supported or encouraged the improvement of churches and halls.

Church going was not only an important Sunday activity, but Bible reading and Bible classes were also encouraged, particularly by Charlotte, who taught such classes. It was Charlotte and her sister who had built the schools at Cross, and funded a number of scholarships.

From the 1850s, Charlotte ran a school at Pentillie Quay, and it is possible that the 'bathing house' was refurbished at that time, for that purpose.

In the tradition of the paternalistic great landowner, they had regular events for tenants, including annual events at Christmas and other feast days. There were balls, parties for people on the estate and even sporting days. Game, money and coals were distributed not just to the tenants but to the poor as well.

Children also had regular 'big' events, with teas and children's entertainers. Charlotte instituted an annual 'Cherry Pie' feast for the children of the estate at the end of the fruit harvest. Fruit had become an important and profitable activity in the valleys around the Tamar.

The obituary reported that Colonel Coryton had been much liked. Certainly the tales that have survived from tenants who lived to report their memories suggest a golden age under a beloved landlord at a time when farming was profitable, and wheat prices high.

I cannot believe that this is the whole story, and suspect that there must have been other activities engaged in by Augustus during this long period of fifty years.

For most of his life his heir was his 4th brother George. George died in 1886, so that the estate went to George's eldest son, William.

For much of the 19thC, there seems to have been little change at Pentillie Castle. The photograph above, taken in the mid 20thC, gives a clear idea of that house, but cannot show the extent of estate buildings, laundries, barns, mills, gardens and workshops, stables, pigsties, quays and woodlands that made Pentillie a village and not just a house. Country houses of the 19thC were devastated by fire, which was seen as an ever abiding risk. These two small survivals from a staff fire operation are not only colourful but evidence of the extent of staff activities at Pentillie.

The pillar box fire centre has engraved on it in black the useful phrase: 'Bucket Fire Extinguisher- Remove cover and lift out 7 buckets full of water'

A wheeled fire engine with pump and hose, for rushing to the source of fire.

Early twentieth century photographs of Pentillie

Pentillie Castle had not changed greatly since it had been rebuilt in 1810. These photographs can therefore give an idea of a house that would have been familiar to John Tillie Coryton.

1. The first picture shows the house from the west, with lawns occupying what was once the outer courtyard garden of Sir James Tillie's house. The courtyard wall in the centre was part of the 1700 building. The wing to the left, which housed the servant's hall and a great kitchen, which early fell out of use, may predate 1810, or use part of an earlier wing.

2. The second picture shows the north side of this wing, with in the distance the west end of the 'chapel' wing.

3. The main courtyard, once a grand entrance to the colonnade of Sir James Tillie, has become an unimportant service area, surrounded by small extensions and blocked windows. Notice the water closet on stilts in the corner. This view looks south-east.

4. The picture of the central courtyard looking north-east shows that the colonnade has become blocked. The statue of Sir James can be made out, obscured by an extension and stuffed against the hidden central pillar.

5. The imposing Gothic mass to the right or south is all by William Wilkins. The front door itself is exceptionally high and overpowering, and the false porte-cochere to the south even more so. This wing had just three main rooms on the ground floor, with lots of corridor, and some inner service areas. This was the wing that was used as a maternity hospital during the second world war, and where the 'Pentillie Babes' were born.

The eastern terrace, not shown on this page, looked over several formal terraces, was imposing and buttressed, but, I suspect, rather depressing.

William Coryton   1847-1919
Country Pursuits and a Family Home

Colonel Augustus Coryton died in 1891, and the estate was inherited by his nephew, William Coryton. Although spending much time at Pentillie from 1870, he had been born in Liss, Hampshire, and had married Evelyn the daughter of Admiral George Parker at Cornwood in Devon, in 1887. For a few years they had a house at Hatt, Saltash, and it was therefore only in 1891 that William and Evelyn moved to Pentillie Castle.

He was not a young man, having been born in 1847, but had a wife with energy, character and what the papers now call a sense of humour. William and Evelyn ushered in a golden age for Pentillie Castle, which lasted almost thirty years.

William Coryton: A charcoal drawing, c 1882

William worked hard on the management of the estate. He was not an absentee landlord, and was recognized as not only a good and caring landlord but also a manager and farmer who was interested in modernizing farming methods.

Among his achievements were the clearing of new fields on Viverdon Down, northwest of St Mellion, which he financed from 1893 when there was a surge of unemployment and poverty following the closing of the Devon Great Consols Mine. He continued with clearance until the government decided to tax such efforts.

He ran a home farm with a large dairy herd (288 in 1898). This was said to have increased to 600 milch cows, a large herd for the time. This required considerable land, and he held and farmed some 1,400 acres in hand.

Enthusiastic for modern techniques, he was one of the first to put his cows in for tubercular testing.

He also established 'The Three Towns Dairy' which, from 1898, only supplied tuberculin tested milk.

William also spent much time and money on the improvement of the farms, in rebuilding cottages and in particular encouraging improvement of land. He was interested in improving the conditions of their families, which included building a shop in Quethiock and financing local schools.

Unusually for the period, he was prepared to reduce rents when times were poor for agriculture, abating farm rents by 10% in 1895, for instance.

Plough teams working on Viverdon Down, north west of St Mellion

At the turn of the century he arranged a large loan to finance 'renovations and repairs to Pentillie and Colebrooke estates', a loan which appears to have required an Act of Parliament to meet the requirements of the trustees. This in turn may, with death duties, have contributed to the sad sale of the farms and village of Quethiock in 1919.

The head gardener, a person of great importance, in his masonic regalia.

His house and the immediate estate was more like a large village with many people, staff, gardeners and farm workers. He appears to have got on well with many, and to continue to maintain and improve the garden. It was he who imported so many plants from America in shipments around 1904, and that part of the garden received the name 'American Garden'. It was not, however, only his gardens that received attention, since parts of his land were also developed for horticulture. William Coryton's great interest was country sports. This included a devotion to energetic country shooting, but above all to hunting. He maintained a house in Devon to be closer to the Dartmoor Hunt, of which he was for many years the Master. Writers of the time noted that for much of his time he maintained the hunt without subscription for 14 years, and did not miss a season for 45 years. A popular master, many relics of the respect in which he was held are still at Pentillie, including the great portrait which was commissioned by 150 of his hunt colleagues.

He also welcomed casual visitors to the castle

A group of hunt followers on east terrace at Pentillie

grounds, making arrangements for his staff to meet steamers coming from Plymouth or Devonport, and landing at Halton Quay.

William Coryton appears to have been a good squire, genuinely liked and respected by his tenants.

Although a great landowner, connected with the great of two counties, the Corytons do not seem to have had that sense of social superiority that could sometimes be found at the time.

Fishing on the river below Pentillie

Nevertheless, they certainly entertained well.

Records of big events are plentiful, starting from the celebrations of their own marriage in 1887. The newspaper reports for this suggest a world it is now difficult to imagine. Not only were the formality and grandeur of the event considerable, but the wedding presents quite magnificent, and given with an eye to show.

The papers published the full list of presents - over 450 of them. This was fine for those many who gave a silver salver, but not so good for those giving a spoon or plate. And why did several different donors give a lamp in the shape of an owl?

Memorable occasions were the parties given when John Tillie Coryton came of age in 1909. These events included days of celebrations for all, including the 600 tenants and their wives.

An early postcard of the river at Pentillie, with a visitors' steamer(?)

The house, a large collection of rooms round one principal and two lesser courtyards, had received minor alterations and improvements, but remained the building designed by Wilkins.

The more spacious rooms and arrangements of Wilkins' design had become divided and somewhat cluttered, with small additions and extensions, such as a first floor water closet on posts. The house itself looks rather grey in many of the photographs that survive. However, this is not what was seen or remembered by visitors. It seems certain that the situation or site, and above all the colourful, interesting gardens and terraces and the fresh cut flowers in every room, made a great impression on all.

The Library

The south terrace

The Drawing room and Library

The grand rooms in the south wing were used largely for entertaining. The dining room was used every day.

These rooms demonstrate the height of overpowering late Victorian fashion.

They look like rooms in which you could only sit up straight, examine conversation pieces or cabinets full of curios.

It is refreshing to read the Coryton children's journal and find that life was not always like that suggested in these pictures.

The Drawing room

Early photographs always show forced, static and humourless subjects. It is difficult to imagine that this houseparty was probably one of laughter and fun.

The second photograph shows a rough shooting party (a Coryton is on the right), which serves to emphasise the importance of shooting in daily life. Shoots were not always organised, but rough rambles that involved hours of country walking.

There seem to have been plenty of sports days. Both hockey and cricket get many mentions, and there was a cricket pitch at Pentillie for weekend play.

William Coryton also saw and enjoyed the change from house and trap to motor car. This picture shows an early trip with chauffeur and a rather nervous family group of mother and the three girls, all well wrapped up, and with waterproof capes over their knees. The car is thought to be a Sunbeam registered to Mr W Coryton in 1906. It has imitation leaf springs printed into the side, which might help identification.

A portrait of William Coryton
by Frank Paton & Cecil Cutler 1900 and presented to William Coryton by his
friends of the hunt. The picture was painted above Harford, Ivybridge, Devon

This poem was written to celebrate William Coryton's birthday in October 1904. It was written for the family magazine by *Nyleve Notyroc*. This reads as Evelyn Coryton if each word is reversed.

This Evelyn was probably his wife rather than his daughter, who shared the same name.

This birthday ode serves as a good summary for a man who seems to have been well liked by family and staff, and famous for his works on both his and his tenants farms.

There is no doubt, however, that his abiding passion was for the hunt. He was Master of the Dartmoor Hunt for many years and had a house near there. Hounds were at Ivybridge and many horses stabled at Pentillie. 150 followers paid for this magnificent large painting to be presented to him.

A Birthday Ode

Hail to William Coryton
Foxhunter of name well known
Since the day that saw his birth
Fifty seven years have flown
Some passed by with sorrow filled
Others brought a healing joy
Years of such like varied moods
Mould the man, from thoughtless boy
Space forbids me now to tell
Of his countless bovine herds
Of his mighty farming works
And his wondrous bags of birds
We wish him power for others good
May health and peace with him abound
Long may he live in happy home
With his children gathered round

Nyleve Notyroc

An Edwardian Family

We are fortunate that Eveleyn and her children, particularly the girls educated at home, wrote about life at Pentillie between 1902 and 1908.

A family newspaper, 'The Merry Magazine', with columns and articles in imitation of a London Newspaper, included a serial in monthly parts called 'Recollections of a Riotous Family, by one of them'.

This tells of the family's life at the Castle during a golden era. It is clear that the girls, in particular, seem to have been happy, and enjoyed good relations with the staff. Indeed, the relationship between staff and family, between tenants and landlords seems more equal and equable than history books might suggest.

The newspaper includes stories of the dreaded Sunday, when not much must happen, and of the formal visiting that society then required. There are also telling remarks about the need to listen to missionary tales. There are stories of entertainments held at the castle, and dances, balls and social events held at neighbours. The boys' life at boarding school and Eton does not get much mentioned. "The Tillie Hut Company" a garden house built by the children, (and, we suspect, the staff) was their own retreat. Here they could entertain and on one occasion, hold a bazaar. There are also tales of games, a lot of mud, and a world that was not risk free. It included, even for the girls, games of hockey and other sports, and hill walking. There is also of course a lot about horses, hunting, dogs and pets, stables, kennels and the health and life of their animals. Some entries remind us that the interests and activities of children never change

through the ages.

It seems that the family had a wicked sense of humour, enjoyed practical jokes, got on well with and respected the staff.

Seen through the children's eyes, this remains an attractive family and group of people. The number of photographs suggests that the children must have had their own camera.

It was probably written largely by the eldest daughter, Ruth Evelyn, perhaps with assistance from her mother. It is not certain who wrote the large number of poems.

Ruth Evelyn was the grandmother of the present owner, Ted Coryton.

Pseudonyms and family nicknames sometimes make it difficult to follow.
The people concerned are:

William Coryton: Father
Born in 1847, he was therefore between 50 and 60 at the time of these stories. Also called 'Mr Wilton' in the journal.

Evelyn Annie Coryton: Mother

John (known as Jack)	born 1888
Edmund George	born 1889
Ruth Evelyn, The author	born 1891
Mary Louisa (?Meg)	born 1893
William Alec	born 1895
Joan Elizabeth Loveday (known as Loveday)	born 1900

"Bentory" was the pseudonym for William Henry Edgcumbe, 4th Earl Edgcumbe, 1832-1917

Here are some short edited extracts, including the report of the unexpected visit by King Edward VII in 1902.

William Coryton 1847-1919
painted 1887

Evelyn Annie Coryton
painted 1898

John Tillie Coryton
painted 1895 aged 7

Edmund George Coryton
painted 1895 age 6

A portrait of a lovely girl,
perhaps Ruth Evelyn

Recollections of a Riotous Family
By One of Them.

We are a large family which Mother says is economical as we can wear out each others clothes. We are really proud at doing that when we are quite young, but as one gets older one begins to think it rather a bore. Father doesn't find a big family economical, tho' he began by wanting fifteen children, now he says he has quite as many as he can manage and is glad, too, they are not all boys, which is what he did want at first.

Mother wishes that some of us were twins, but she says that she can pretend that Rose and Meg are since they are so much of the same size. Mother is very fond of pretending, she says it helps you to ever so many things you can't have otherwise - so we all pretend a good deal, even Loveday the youngest who is only five and a great pet with all of us: she plays hockey, football and cricket, quite by herself and gets very hot and excited over it, she knocks the ball about the ground first, - "keeping warm", she explains, "till the other side comes" - then she hits off quite correctly and scores goal after goal. Mother told her the sides could not be fairly divided, as it seemed rather hard that the other side never won - she quite saw that and said she would make it all right by being the other side herself.

There was a garden missionary meeting one day, but only Meg would go with Mother, because she was the only one who did not know what it would be like. The Missionary was a black man, and Meg did not like having to shake hands with him at all, tho' she did want very much to see his tongue, to make sure if it was black too.

Photos of Father, Mother and all six children.

Whilst they were all waiting for the black man to begin talking, two ducks waddled in front of everybody, and one laid an egg. "The first contribution" someone said, but unluckily the other duck gobbled it up.

Everybody laughed a great deal, but Mother says missionary meetings are usually amusing tho' she isn't sure that they are intended to be.

Holidays

We are always glad when the holidays come and we generally have an opening celebration of some sort.

We go to the dentist in the holidays too. He is kind and tells us we are brave so of course we are, but we try to go there just before his lunchtime, then he doesn't find nearly so many holes to mend.

The last time three of us went, Meg and Arthur bought two tortoises in the street, they were sixpence each. One died the same evening, and the other we gave to the gardener next day as he wanted something to eat the slugs and woodlice in the hothouses. ......it seemed rather quiet for us but the gardener is older. We offered it to Mother but she says she is the wrong age too for tortoises.

When Loveday was vaccinated we all went to see that. Arthur chose it as his special treat to make up for not going to a village concert.

On wet days in the holidays we camp out in the woods with the ponies as that doesn't waste the fine days. If Rose has to hold a horse in the rain, she pretends to be a cabman and that makes her quite happy even when its very cold and she is wet through.

Quiet on Sundays

We were fond at playing at real farmyards and one Sunday we were all different animals, Rose was a cow, and Arthur was a calf; but he spoilt it all by crying dreadfully, because he wanted to be a bull calf, and the others wouldn't let him.
Mother had thought it a nice quiet game for Sunday as we used to be tied up with some grass in front of us for a long time, so Arthur's making such a fuss about being a heifer calf, was very disappointing.

Another quiet game was laying buttons; we sat on a button for five minutes and we might not speak or move. Then when Mother lifted us off our seats she would find two buttons. But we liked laying half-pennies best, as buttons were not much use to us - and Arthur wanted to lay a gold watch. He asked Mother if it would be very hard work, and she said yes, he'd have to sit still all day and all night. That made him give up the idea.

Some visitors were shown in once when Mother was writing letters, and three of us were laying half-pennies, of course we could not even say 'How do you do'. They seemed to think it rather a funny game but one of them said she should teach it to her children.

The Garden Hut Company

We have a hut, which we built ourselves mostly. ... Our hut has a drawing room, that was built first, then the stables and last the kitchen.

We can cook quite well at our kitchen fire; and on Mother's birthday our treat was to have the butler to tea with us at the Hut. He is called Charkins and has been ever so many years with us, he is so amusing and never seems to mind what we do, and his hair is all white and grey, like Mother's, so we like him very much. When he had tea with us, we gave him scrambled eggs, he told Mother after, how much he enjoyed himself, and that the scrambled eggs were very tasty; Mother said he worded his praise most skilfully.

Charkins enjoys scrambled eggs at the Hut

Getting dirty

It took us some time to furnish our Hut properly, ... but Meg was the one who did most towards the furnishing. She used to poke about in the ash pits and rubbish heaps and it was surprising what capital things she got, enamel dishes, iron cooking spoons and kettles - they all wanted mending - but we soon got that done. Nurse rather tried to prevent Meg ferreting about like this as it seemed to make her more grubby than the rest of us, but Mother begged her not to discourage archaeological and antiquarian research.
We used to have special days in the week, that we called "Dirty Days" when we could get as messy as we

pleased, because our frocks went to the wash next day. How we did like "Dirty Days", and used to beg for tea by the river then, when the mud is black and slimey and we could not help getting in a mess.

A Bazaar in the Hut

Of course our building operations gave us a good deal of expense, as we had to buy tools, and also wanted to give presents to the workmen who were kind enough to help us in their dinner hour. So Jeffery who is capital at thinking of things, tho' he doesn't do so much as the others, said we must have a Bazaar, that everybody got money by Bazaars; and he went round getting things to sell. He found lots of nice useful things in the nursery, button hooks, shoe horns, hair brushes, and bootlaces which he even took out of the boots.

Nurse

Nurse was rather cross at first, but afterwards she was quite nice about it and went to the Bazaar early in order to buy them all back again....

It was Jeffery who said he could not possibly have a Bazaar without a Band, that people never did; and he bothered Mother so about it, that she sent round the house to find out who could play any instrument whatever, she found that Charkins could play the concertina, James (the groom) accordion and a cousin of ours called Violet, said she and one of the housemaids would play on combs in parts, and they did it very well. Mother discovered an old big drum in the lumber room, which once belonged to a brass band, and after a great deal of trouble she persuaded the valet to play that, he seemed rather shy about it - then Mother promised she'd play the penny whistle (tho' here is a shilling one); and that was all settled, when next Jeffery said that of course there must be a tea, so we had a grand tea in the wood. Tables and benches just like a real bazaar, only a much better tea. You paid 2d. for tea, and that admitted you to the Hut where the sale was held, as well. All the servants came, and the people from the cottages close to the house. The housekeeper

poured out tea, with Auntie and Father sitting beside her, and every one enjoyed it tremendously. The band played nearly all the time. Charkins generally played *Rule Britannia*, and the combs tried to play whatever Charkins did. James was best at dance music, but he got on a little with Rule Britannia now and then, only unluckily his accordion was not tuned to the same pitch as the concertina. Mother can play heaps of tunes on her whistle, but <u>not</u> *Rule Britannia*, or *Dances*, so she just played what she liked and came in when she could; anyhow she was laughing so much that she could mostly only blow squeaks. But the big drum was splendid, it never stopped, kept time so well and made it all blend, so Mother said. They finished quite properly with *God Save the Queen*; Mother can play all that except one note which is too low.

We made a lot of money, over £3. It took a long time to sell everything, because only four people including the sellers could fit into the Hut at the same time. Father bought everything at the end that nobody else wanted to buy.

Since that time we have really grand furniture in our Hut and a visitors book which is full of names. We have some quite celebrated ones. Sir Reginald Pole Carew and some Admirals, besides all our own and the carpenters and sawyers and everybody on the place almost. We are so sorry we have not got the King's but we never thought of a visitors book till after he came here and wrote his name in Mother's but perhaps it is a good thing we did not show him our Hut - he would not have known that when he sat on any of the chairs he must hold on to the table.

The Schoolroom.
Once the principal *salon* and now the dining room

The King's Visit

The King's visit.... is really the most important of all our recollections - and it was all the greater event to us, because it happened on a Sunday. Father likes a very strict Sunday, and Mother a very peaceful one, so if any thing happens on a Sunday it makes a great impression on all of us.

Nurse heard at church that Lord Bentory, who is a neighbour of ours, was going to bring the King up the river, to see a dear old house (Cotehele) he has 3 miles above ours. So directly after luncheon we were all on the look out, then someone called from the nursery window "He's coming" but all we could see was a very big timber barge with masts, being towed up - the barge did look very clean and with all the brass polished and shining in the sun, but mother said she was quite sure the King would not come in that nor so early either. However we children all went down to the quay, and found quite a little crowd collecting there.

We had several false alarms, but at last after Mother, with Loveday (who was only a baby in her mail cart) came down, we saw a steam launch coming. Mother told the boys to be sure to take off their hats, and the girls to curtsey and as the boat went by we did as we were told, and Mother made her best curtsey - but there was no King there - they were only the servants going up to get the tea ready. They were quite kind, only smiled, touched their hats and said the King would be up about four. Then Mother said there was no doubt about it now, and Father must come down. So some of us ran up and dug him out of his office where he was very busy (as Jeffers, when a tiny boy once said) having his Sunday nap.

Well we waited and waited - but at last we heard distant cheers from a place lower down the river, and then the launch came round the bend and there was the King sitting in the stern. We all did our curtseys again as they came near; we noticed how the boat hugged our shore and as she neared the quay Lord Bentory came to the bows and called out "Is Mr. Wilton at home?" There was no answer, for Father thought he would not be noticed if he did not speak. So Lord Bentory repeated his question - Mother then stepped forward and said "Yes, he's here", "The King would like to land - about six; and please send a carriage" shouted Lord Bentory.

"All right", mother called back, and they were gone again, Mother wishing she had said something prettier than "All right".

Then there was such excitement, all the people delighted, Father wishing the earth would open up and swallow him, and that he had not been persuaded to come down to the quay; but he soon began thinking about the carriage and arranging everything, the coachman was at the quay looking on, so he went off to get ready, and we all started for the house. On the way up we met some friends who had come to spend the afternoon - they told us after they could see at once that something important had happened, and that they would not have missed the whole excitement, especially the discussion about Father's clothes, for anything.

What to wear?

They thought Father could wear ordinary clothes, as the King and everybody else would be in yachting dress. Father was very firm that this was an occasion when he would rather be over dressed than under dressed, and so his frock coat and top hat were most suitable he considered. Mother was very glad he thought of the frock coat as she had given it to him some time before, but he would not wear it, as he felt too smart in it; and Mother always said she knew it would be put by till her funeral, when he would put it on in memory of her and not to hurt her feelings. They finally, after talking a good deal about it, consulted Charkins, and he decided on the frock coat, top hat, and wedding trousers, so that quite settled it all.

Father and Charkins decide on the frock coat,
top hat and wedding trousers.

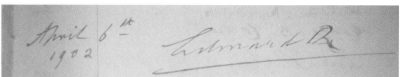

The housekeeper contributed her share to the grandeur of the occasion by running about looking for mats to cover the holes in the passage carpet.

We had tea, and Mother lent her friend a tidy pair of gloves, then we were all ready and waiting long before the launch came back again. That waiting was rather dreadful, we all began to feel jumpy, tho' Mother said the King knew quite well she did not often receive Royalty, and so he would not mind if she did not do everything quite correctly; and when at last he came everything seemed as easy as possible.

Father and Mother had wondered if they would have to kiss his hand, but he settled that by shaking hands at once - and saying he was sorry to be late - then he shook hands with us, we all stood in a row and Rose wondered why a King who could do what he liked, wore gloves. Then he turned to Mother and said something to her about the beautiful gardens he had heard of, so Mother was able to ask him to drive up and see them. He told her to get in first and where to sit; and then Father and Lord Bentory got in too. Mother told us after she could not help being amused when they got to the avenue gate, where they were to get out and walk. When the footman opened the door, Father was so anxious to let the King be first, that he sat still himself, so the King got out and helped Mother; but really Father ought to have been before hand and handed him out, especially as he was very lame having hurt his knee not long before. They walked up to the middle of the shrubbery garden, where there were any number of rhododendrons in full bloom, and met us.

We children had brought all the courtiers, as Guy called them, up the garden path from the Quay - they were rather sorry for themselves when climbing up, as it is so steep, but after they said, it was quite worth it to see such wonderful flowers. We met Mother's party and all stood and talked.

Lord Bentory asked Rose why she did not bring out her soldiers as a guard of honour for the King - for he knew about Rose's army. Rose said "Because they were so silly, they wouldn't keep serious". The King heard this and wanted to know more, so Mother told him about the army which consisted of all the maid servants - and how she used to drill them, and give them rations of lemonade and apples; also that one day she had a big review by the front door, marched them all round the green, then all sang God Save the King and were dismissed to barracks, and the best part of the story was that Rose sent a message to General Pole Carew to say that she had had a review and she wished he had been there, he would have been so very useful to her. How the King and the Courtiers did laugh at that; and more still when Rose added "We drill always on Saturdays because it is the laundry maids' half holiday". The King asked Rose if she knew any words of command.

Lord Bentory was rather in a fuss to be off now on account of the tide, it would never do for a King to be stuck in the mud like lots of people are, even Lord Bentory has been, so we all moved down to the house and round the terrace to see the view. Then Mother summoned up courage to ask the King to write his name in the visitors' book, she was going to bring it out to him, but he followed her in thro' the window; of course he asked for a J pen and there was not one; but he wrote quite well without it.

Father took him to see the pictures in the dining room and Mother and Lord Bentory had quite a rush to get back to the carriage as they suddenly were told the King was waiting for them, didn't they run!

Now we all began the procession back to the quay. We had two or three courtiers a-piece to talk to, but luckily most of them were very jolly, and did all the talking. When we got to the quay we found that the crowd had grown bigger. Nurse too had gone about getting people to sing "God Save the King"; so when we had done all our goodbyes and the boat was ready to start, they struck up - the policeman and our farm hind started it. It was a little quavery at first, but it ended splendidly and the boat steamed away.

Then slowly and sadly we went back to the house - Guy sat down and said he couldn't really believe he had just been talking to the King - oh dear! we did feel sorry to think it was all over - even Father liked it very much, the King was so kind and friendly; one of our farm men said "He was a proper jolly fellow and not a bit what we expected to see him".

Pictures of the children & their activities.

Four photos marked to show the four seasons of spring, summer, autumn and winter. Identify the four seasons.

Follies, Garden and Estate buildings

The house has approximately 55 acres of garden, and a further two hundred acres was landscaped to form part of the setting. In this area are many buildings which provided services. These include stables, cow byres, staff cottages, sawmills, and many other buildings. They are of various ages and styles, with the oldest having been erected by Sir James Tillie around 1690.

There is also plenty of confusion as to dates, since many re-use old stones. Some of this 15th & 16thC stone came from demolished houses. We know that the old house at Pentearr, near the outer gates was demolished, as, in the early 19thC, were the mansions at Clifton and at Crocadon. Some stones may also have come from demolition when the 1810 wing was built, or from the demolition of that wing in 1978.

One of the intriguing elements of research at Pentillie is the sheer quantity of well cut stone, roll moulded door jambs, columns, window mullions cills, fireplaces, and so on. They not only fill the gardens of Pentillie but can be seen throughout the buildings of the estate. In just four lesser buildings one can count some 15 granite doorways from the early 16thC and 13 mullioned stone windows. The steps in the garden themselves are re-used sections from a once high-status build.

The 'spare' stones include parts of a Tillie column whose original position is unknown. One notable red herring is at the entrance to the Lime Avenue, where gates have a datestone alongside them reading *NLEL 1628*.

Just south of Pentillie, on the edge of the river, was a substantial medieval mansion, with medieval quay, halls and a private chapel. Clifton was the home of the Lower family, which was once of distinction and importance. Sir Nicholas Lower, a descendant of the Arundell and Killigrew families, married in 1628 Elizabeth who had already been twice widowed. He was knighted by Charles I, served a term as Sheriff of Cornwall, and his life features in histories of the period. Their tombs are in Landulph Church. Clifton's chief claim to fame has always been that Nicholas provided lodging for *Theodorus Paleolugius*, from Mystra who claimed with some justification to be the legal descendant of the last emperor of Byzantine.

That has to be worth marks in a pub quiz.

Clifton was bought in the mid 19thC, when the buildings were removed and a new farmhouse built in its place. The stone NLEL probably commemorates the marriage of Nicholas and Elizabeth and comes from Clifton.

We know that Sir James Tillie started re-building his house by using three stone doorways from another house, cutting his own name and date into the stone above the decoration. Re-use is an honourable and sensible trait.

In addition to service buildings, there are also many ornamental garden and estate buildings. A schedule of the remnants lists some 100 follies or buildings, many now almost vanished.

It is only possible to give a taster of the many splendid buildings around the house and garden particularly as the follies, seats, well houses, and towers are still difficult to photograph, as is the 17thC walling and the 18thC stables.

However, we can start with the 18thC granary standing on its toadstools north of the house.

This building design for keeping corn dry and rat free, was once common. It is increasingly difficult to find good examples.

Equally important survivals are the utility buildings, of which this small well head is one.

The most glamorous 'other' building is undoubtedly the Mausoleum, which has been described elsewhere.

Just as interesting to the historian are the lesser buildings and their often striking designs.

The kitchen garden at Pentillie is of considerable size, with potting shed, glass houses, cottages and so on. This garden also has a 'bell' door, so called because it rang, if opened, to warn of family entry. Contrary to normal building practice, the wall, which is faced with stone to the outerside and brick to the inner, with brick jambs, quoins and lintels, is built to follow the slope of the land. It has survived about 160 years, and still looks good. It is an architectural wonder.

Two pictures of 'The Bell Door' to the kitchen garden

There are so many small buildings, cottages and ornaments to the garden and estate that is difficult to make a choice. A delightful building is this 19thC chapel at Halton, part of an old manor and quay bought in 1869.

Even the old well was prettied up and given a fine new entrance.

Another group of interest are the houses by the entrance.

These include Stockadon Villa, built opposite the previous entrance to Pentillie as the estate office. This is a fine Regency villa, with two detached pavilions joined to the house by screen wall; one held horses, the other staff.

In 1877 a writer described it as *Palladio's villa plan 'en miniature'. The first floor verandah is a nice English enrichment of Palladio. (Luckhurst).*

The prettiest building on the estate is probably the Bathing Hut. Whether looking down from above, from the banks or from the water, this is a satisfying little building. It may originally have been an 18thC quay building, but by 1855 had been reconstructed. It was used as a school by Charlotte Coryton.

It has everything a Disney designer could ask for. The re-used earlier stonework is of quality; the Victorian detailing of the internal eaves is clever and practical; the chimney is nicely detailed; the fireplace is from an earlier house of status. Now used for entertaining, this is a splendid building.

It forms part of a riverside group, much rebuilt in the 19thC, with a stone quay and the remnants of lime kilns, which themselves had castellated entrances.

The group, which includes the 'lodge', was built roughly in line with Repton's recommendations, and was a good attempt at re-creating a vision of the past, probably carried out when Wilkins had completed extending the house in 1810.

They re-use much old stone to create a confused but romantic Gothic vision at the entrance to Pentillie.

The Lodge at the entrance to Pentillie Castle

Churches and memorials

It is only in the last century that the local church has lost its connection to the 'big' house. Two churches are associated with the Coryton Family.

Pillaton Church is about three miles to the west and St Mellion Church about a mile to the north-west. The families have been connected to both parishes, not only through their former house at West Newton Ferrers, but also because of their time at Crocadon, St Mellion. Pentillie itself is now in St Mellion, but is right on the boundary between the two parishes.

There are several Coryton memorials in Pillaton Church which is on a Celtic mound by a cross roads just in from the river. It is worth a visit. Not only is this a lovely church but it is also next to a pub (a former church house) that claims foundation from medieval times.

St Mellion Church was dedicated by Bishop Bronescombe in 1259 and is of 14th and 15thC date. It also has a fine Jacobean pulpit. In the 19thC, repair and remodelling of the church was partially financed by the Corytons.

However, the glories of the church are the Coryton monuments.

First, reset brass plates on the south wall attest to Peter Coryton (d.1500), his wife and their 24 children.

I counted 14 Coryton monuments in the church, many a reminder of lives spent in service or war overseas.

Overshadowing the interior of the church are two magnificent canopied monuments.

The brass to Peter Coryton and his numerous family.

In the north-east corner, to one side of a helmet which is itself a monument, is the tomb of William Coryton (d. 1651) and his wife Elizabeth (d. 1656). This was the William Coryton who, as described on page 9, stood as one of three against the king. This, a wonderful piece of work, and typical of its time, is pictured on the next page.

St Mellion Church

Photographs of the monument of William Coryton (d. 1651) and his wife Elizabeth (d. 1656)

Sadly it is difficult to stand back and take in the full glory of this ornate monument which includes much strapwork, Jacobean detailing, angels, and a magnificent coat of arms. William and Elizabeth are shown kneeling to a prie-dieu. A slate memorial gives their details, a Latin paragraph, and a poem. The monument was raised by their son John, so this verse may be by him.

> This Marble Pile is placed on
> The thrice Renowned Coryton:
> (But his owne Name, a Trophie, shall
> Out-last this his Memoriall.)
> Grave, Wise, and Pious: Heav'n him lent
> To be his Ages President.
> Both Good and Great; and yet Belov'd.
> In judgements just, in trust's Approu'd
> Honour'd by th' Offices he bore
> In Publique: but by's Meeknesse more.
> Loyall in Warre, in peace he stood
> The Pillar of the Common-good.
> Wordes may not set his prayses foorth,
> Nor Prayses comprehend his worth:
> His Worth doth speake him thus, in briefe,
> Cornwalls late Glory, now it's Griefe.

A fine sentiment, even if not great poetry.

The decoration on this earlier monument is worth comparing with that of a similarly magnificent monument which is only some fifty years later, but which encapsulates the change in taste that had taken place.

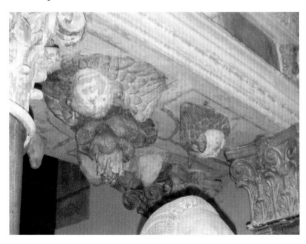

A detail from the decoration of the
1651 Coryton Monument

At the east end of the north aisle is a monument to the later Sir William Coryton (d 1711) and his first wife Susannah (d 1695).

This also has coats of arms, blazons and decorations.

The married couple, shown in the costume of the day, are kneeling each side of a prie-dieu. It is interesting that, presumably for matters of dynastic pride, Sir William chose to be remembered with his first, rather than his second wife.

The pillars stand on a deep decorated base which was obscured, and therefore does not show in the photograph.

Photographs of the monument to the later Sir William (d 1711) and his wife Susannah (d 1695).

The 20th Century: John Coryton 1888-1965

After William Coryton's death in 1919 his eldest son John inherited.

The first event was the sale of the many farms and village of Quethiock. This was a disaster for the tenants, but may have been necessary to meet tax demands and, in October 1920, to repay the loan which William's trustees had taken out in 1903 to fund estate improvements.

John (known as Jack) had married Dorothy Parker in 1916, having met her while recovering from a head wound. They had two sons and a daughter.

Jack Coryton, 'JP and squire of Pentillie with its many tenants and broad acres of farms and woods' was affectionately remembered. A man of military directness, he was also a man of rages, perhaps the result of that head wound received during the First World War. Jack continued the life of a great squire with large house and estate. He continued to farm and was a keen breeder of cattle and pigs.

Jack and Dorothy always lived in some style. They were hospitable, enjoyed the company of guests and always changed for dinner.

From about 1940 on, however, they ate in the old schoolroom (now the dining room) as more intimate than the great dining room and requiring few if any servants, most having been lost to war service. They still had a chauffeur, Fowler, who had a service exemption. He was therefore important to the establishment, although he and Jack very often disagreed. Small gains were the arrival of prisoners of war to pick potatoes in 1943 and the supply of pit props for the mining industry during the war. At one time, during a farming depression, Jack had taken a job in London and after the war became involved in a milk business. Jack took great interest in the estate, in forestry, in farming and in his own herd of South Devons, but did not enjoy being responsible to his trustees.

Life changed for Jack and Dorothy when their eldest, favourite son, Peter, died in Egypt in 1942.

It was sad that they made no secret of their dismay nor that the second son, Jeffrey, was not a favourite, nor that he had a childless and therefore heirless marriage to Kit, for whom they did not disguise their dislike.

The packet of 'effects' sent to his parents in August 1942 after the death of Peter Coryton is preserved at Pentillie.

During the Second World War, a wing, despite lacking most amenities, was used as a maternity ward, providing an element of safety for Plymouth mothers. Around 180 'Pentillie Babes' have been traced so far, most born in the period 1941-1945.

During the twenty years that followed the war, Jack seemed to lose heart in maintenance, and in planning for the future. All families have disputes, but his sadness and his difficulty in working with trustees meant that the future got overlooked.

Jack and Dorothy enjoyed visits from their extended family, and towards the end of his life a swimming pool was built for the two children of their eldest child, Anne.

Jack died in 1965. His wife Dorothy left to live in London and never visited the castle again.

Hunting continued to be enjoyed by Captain Jack Coryton, who was a keen
supporter of the Dartmoor Hunt.

The house from the air in the 1960s, before demolition.

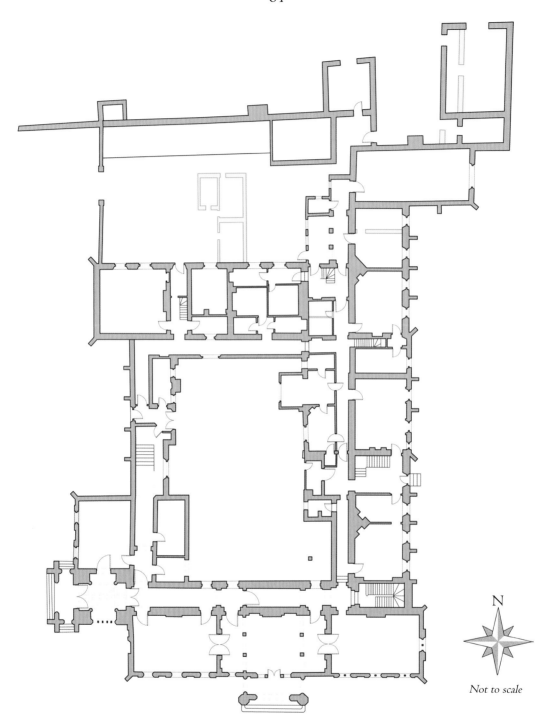

A plan of Pentillie Castle as it was in 1966, before Demolition

The building laid out by William Wilkins in 1812 remained much as it had been built, save for the minor alterations of 150 years. The range built by Sir James Tillie can still be traced, but his Tuscan pillars have been bricked in, and an accumulation of small service buildings has given the courtyard a cluttered look and feel. The kitchens have been moved again and other changes reflect the post-war absence of staff. Other alterations include room divisions, corridors, and additions such as a first floor lavatory on stilts.

N

Not to scale

Jeffery Coryton and Demolition (1922-1980)

Jack's younger son, Jeffery, and his wife Kit, inherited a castle where much work was needed.

Jeffery Coryton had served with distinction in the army and gained the Military Cross in Belgium in 1944, where his 'determination and calm leadership' were praised. Jeffery was considered to be kindly and, having won a 'good' MC in the war, unquestionably brave.

He had no experience and little ability as a farmer or estate manager since he had worked in the City of London since the war. When he inherited, he relied on a land agent to run the estate, an arrangement that is seldom efficient or as satisfactory for tenants or owners, as an estate where the owner is closely involved in the management.

The house, where so much needed to be done, and round which Jeffery and Kit rattled, became an overwhelming problem at a time when, up and down the country, large wings, country houses, and great buildings were being demolished as uneconomic. The decision to demolish has to be seen in the context of views held at the time on large country houses, their future, and their expense. Demolition may have been a choice 'of the time' but it was one that had the support of most. It was said there was only one bathroom for 18 bedrooms, and a dining room an exceptionally long way from the kitchen and no staff to help with the house. There was then no enthusiasm for re-use or development.

Demolition

Jeffery Coryton and Kit decided to demolish almost all the work completed in 1810 and, after some debate, the north service wing also.

This had some interesting results. The pillars that formed so important a part of Sir James Tillie's design were re-discovered and re-instated as part of the design.

Two new pavilions were built beyond each of the two Tillie towers, which was in the spirit of the original design. Some of the 1810 work was saved to make a new *porte cochere* on the south front.

The resulting house, only really one room thick, was almost small, and certainly manageable. It also reflected and retained much of Sir James Tillie's original design.

Pictures of the 1966 demolition, including the finding of the granite colonnade.

The house reduced in size: circa 1980

Pentillie after demolition and rebuild in 1968.
The new pavilions and porte-cochere are shown
hatched.

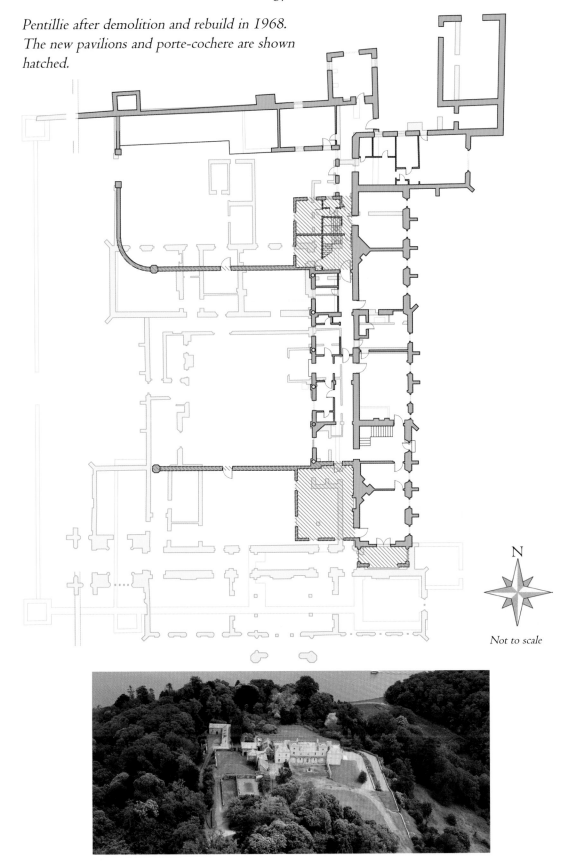

N

Not to scale

Planning for the 21st century.

Once the size of the main house was reduced, Jeffery had to consider what might happen after his death, since he and Kit had no children.

In 1977, at a time when several farm tenants were retiring, he asked his first cousin, Ted Spencer to come and talk about taking on the vacant farmland and gradually taking over the estate from the agent. Ted Spencer, who was in his early thirties, had married Sarah Dewhurst in 1974, and they now had two infant children. He was running a helicopter company in Scotland.

This was quite a change and challenge but, against the advice of his own family, Ted Spencer decided to make the break. He started by spending six months working on a farm and followed this with a year's training course in 1979.

Partnership agreements were then agreed and Ted moved to a farm on the estate, which he renovated.

However, Jeffery died unexpectedly in 1980, aged only 57 years.

He had not completed the proposed paperwork and the situation was inevitably complicated by conflicting interests, which included those of the land agent running the estate.

The planned succession did not go smoothly.

Jeffery's wife Kit became the life tenant of the estate. She also, on the advice of her agent, cancelled the farm partnership arrangement made with Ted Spencer, leaving him in an awkward situation.

For the next 27 years, Kit Coryton withdrew into the castle. She was looked after by her chef, Roger Langsford, who lived in the castle and cared for her until her death in September 2007.

Although Jeffery had made Ted his heir, this included a requirement that he should change his name to Coryton, copying events that had already occurred twice in the history of the Coryton family and Pentillie Castle. Despite this change, which carried its own family problems, and despite being charged with trying to continue with the estate, Kit did not welcome Ted, his wife Sarah or his three children, Sammie, Oliver and Roonie. The three children had never been down the driveway of Pentillie until after Kit's death.

Ted, Sarah and his family continued to live just one and a half miles away, working one of the estate farms, and continuing with work in the helicopter business.

This isolation from the life and activities of the estate made it more difficult for the Coryton family to decide what to do when Kit died. They themselves said that they had:

'done a convincing imitation of an ostrich and had refused to consider the eventual problems that would inevitably occur on Kit's death'.

When Kit died, Ted was working in Mauritania. The eldest daughter, Sammie had been living and working in Australia for some years. It was not until Christmas Eve 2007 that the family could meet to discuss the future. They *'locked the door and disconnected the telephone'.* Both parents and the three children were surprised by how Pentillie had 'grabbed' them. They decided together to try and retain the castle and main part of the estate for the family.

They also decided to establish a business that would pay for repairs and improvements.

The whole family being involved in this decision, Ted, Sarah and Sammie decided to devote all their working hours to the project.

A Future.

The Coryton family decided not to sell just to enjoy some good holidays and a few luxuries, but rather to try and find the inheritance tax due. They also decided to renovate the house and to restore the gardens so that they would return to being the centre of a profitable estate.

Two 'retired' architect friends, who were living close by, volunteered to prepare plans for re-modeling the house. This provided for nine bedrooms with en-suite bathrooms, and all the necessary reception rooms, service areas and staff quarters to allow Pentillie Castle to be opened for guests.

Work proceeded fast. It was not just the house that needed work. The gardens had become overgrown, and their extent unkown. This was a family project and the family worked at clearing trees, with friends coming down for regular 'barbecue' clearance weekends.

Plans and planning permission, listed building consent and a wedding licence had to be obtained, and contractors found to carry out the works.

After Kit's death much of the family furniture, interior fittings and contents had been dispersed. This had therefore to be traced, purchased or replaced. Basic facilities had to be modernised, which included new water treatment and storage, re-wiring, and re-designed heating systems.

It was not enough just to renovate, but plans were also necessary to establish a money-earning business.

They worked at speed, helped by their ability to assemble a good team and the enthusiasm that all seemed to have for the project. Such work is never fast enough and can seem unending. However much was achieved in a short time. For instance, I was astonished by the work to clear scrub and suckers, and by the fitting out and carpeting of a basement area as billiard and television room in only five days.

Ollie, Sammie, Sarah, Roonie and Ted Coryton

The house was re-opened and earning money just over a year later, in June 2009.

Perhaps because the house and estate had become little known over the previous thirty years, Pentillie attracted attention.

The efforts of the family also featured in a television series. Nobly endured, this gained good publicity and assisted plans for a successful future.

The house remains a continuing commitment for the whole family, and it is hoped will remain a family house for the future.

Part of The Entrance Hall

The Dining Room

The 'Pentillie Babes', and their parents, in a celebration: May 2009

The interior of Pentillie is now refurbished and is smart, practical and stylish. Even the lead statue of Sir James Tillie that stands outside the entrance has been repaired and remounted.

In their first year, events included garden tours, sports events, dinners, weddings, tours, river parties, lectures, fairs. Many thousands of visitors have now been able to come to Pentillie for the first time. One party was hosted for all those born at Pentillie during the second world war.

The 'Pentillie Babes' and their relatives enjoyed their welcome.

However, Pentillie Castle does not have the atmosphere of a great events centre, hotel or stately home, but rather, remains the home and centre of the Coryton family their friends and estate.

The house is full of reminders from their history. A stick stand in the hall is full of walking sticks, shooting sticks, a stick drinking flask, two foils, and many swords.

The swords are from the six generations of service in the armed forces, a tradition of service that continues. Oliver Coryton has, in 2009, just returned from a tour in Afghanistan.

Pentillie Castle remains a family affair, but encouraged by magnificent and loyal support from friends. It is all the more interesting for that.

It is good to see, also in the hall, that dogs are still part of the family and that they deserve good quality drinking bowls.

The gardens, which cover some fifty five acres and encompass over three hundred years of garden planning, remain relatively unknown. They offer lots of exciting future projects. It is not just the restoration of the walled gardens, the green houses and other buildings, but the many small garden follies, the miles of walks, the shrubs, beds and features that have become hidden over recent decades. Much of this is daunting.

However, the gardens, the dramatic river and landscape remain the important features of Pentillie. There is already much to admire and yet more to which to look forward.

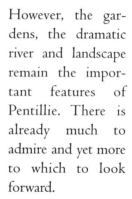

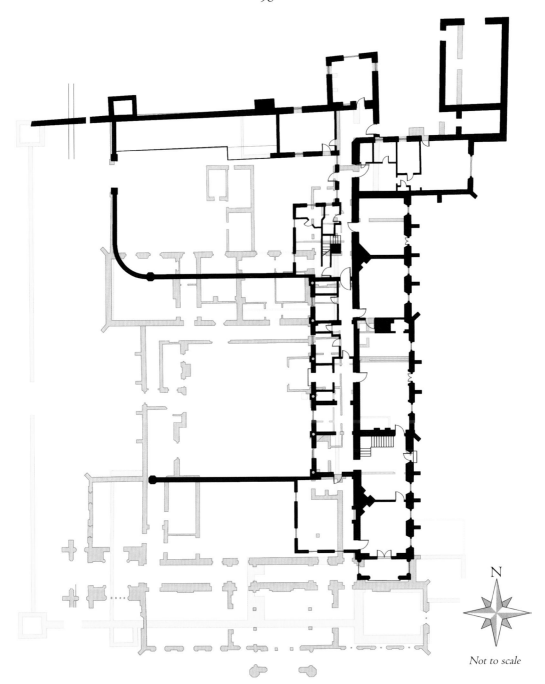

A ground floor plan of Pentillie Castle in 2009

In 2008 plans were drawn up to renovate and modernise Pentillie Castle. The works included new services, a magnificent water system, new floors, structural steel and alterations to the room layout. Bathrooms and facilities that made the Castle suitable for guests and the services they require were provided. The basement was also brought in to use and includes a games room; this floor remains almost entirely the work of Sir James Tillie.

The plan differences appear relatively minor, although the extent of the works and renovation was considerable. The current Castle represents perhaps only one third of the earlier building. The blue background plan is that of 1867, and provided for comparison.

The Pentillie Starter

Handed down through the generations, the 'Pentillie Starter' was a reliable standby for meals at Pentillie Castle. It is still in use today.

If you wish to serve 5-6 people, you will need:

> 4 hard-boiled eggs (one for decoration).
> ½ pint double cream.
> ¼ pint aspic jelly.
> 2 teaspoons Worcester sauce.
> 2 teaspoons essence of anchovies.
> 1 flat teaspoon curry powder.
> Salt and pepper to taste.

Aspic jelly is based on meat stock. There are many recipes for this on the internet.

The recipe uses the old fashioned measure, a 'gill'. which is equal to a quarter of a pint.

Although sometimes disparagingly called 'The Cold Egg Dish', this recipe makes a tasty, easy course with a touch of the special. The recipe for the Pentillie Starter has survived because it was a simple but acceptable good old stand-by dish.

Aspic Jelly:

The jelly is made using one gill of boiling water to one full dessertspoon of jelly powder. You will need either to have made some aspic jelly the day before or you can make it the same day as long as it is allowed to cool but not set.

The Preparation

1. Take the yolks of three hard-boiled eggs.
2. Mash them with Worcester sauce, anchovy essence, curry powder, salt and pepper.
3. Beat the aspic jelly
4. Chop up white of eggs, mix with yolks etc.
5. Beat cream not too stiff, fold in, together with the jelly.
6. Leave in the refrigerator at least an hour to set.

Serving

Serve in a shallow dish decorated with the fourth hard-boiled egg cut into slices, the whole on a bed of rocket or lettuce.

If you are preparing this recipe from available supplies and for modern taste, you can use leaf gelatine and a tasty beef stock or *Maggi's* flavouring for the aspic jelly. Anchovies are available as 'Anchovy Sauce'. We suggest you **reduce** the amount of cream and **increase** the anchovy sauce, Worcester sauce and curry powder, to taste. Serve in very small portions.

Summary of sources and references:

Thanks are given to all those mentioned below for the information they have provided, with particular thanks to Mr and Mrs Ted Coryton and family.

Books on the history and domestic architecture of Cornwall are not included in the short list below.
Further research is necessary in the papers of the Coryton Family and of the Cornwall, Devon or Wiltshire Record Offices and on the medieval and archaeological history of the area.

The Survey of Cornwall   Richard **Carew** of Antonie, esq 1602
Topographical Drawings: Edmund **Prideaux** (1693-1745) Reproduced by permission of Mr & Mrs P Prideaux-Brune
Parochial Histories by William **Hals** (1655-1737) unpublished 1737 Thomas **Tonkin,** (1680-1742) unpublished 1742,
The Parochial History of Cornwall by Davies **Gilbert** 1838
The Gentleman's Magazine for 1791
Biographical History of England **Rev J Granger and Rev Mark Noble**   London 1806
Humphry **Repton** Red Book for Pentillie 1810 Private Collection
Lewis **Kennedy** Proposals for Pentillie (1813) Private Collection
D & S **Lyson's** Parochial History (1814) Cornwall (Volume III for Cornwall)
An Historical Survey of Cornwall by CS **Gilbert** 2 vols   1817 & 1820
Thomas **Moule** The English Counties Delineated: or, A Topographical Description of England,   1838
Lake's Parochial History of Cornwall written by Joseph Polsue c 1865-1872 4 volumes
Cornish Characters and Strange Events **S.Baring-Gould** MA   Two Volumes 1908
Charles **Henderson** Royal Institution of Cornwall Henderson Papers
Plans prepared by Trenwith, Wills & Wills, Chartered Architects London 1966/7
A Victorian Village   A Record of the Parish of Quethiock in Cornwall **Mary French** Glasney Press, Falmouth   1977
Howard **Colvin** A Biographical Dictionary of British Architects 1600-1840 (3rd edition) 1995 Yale UP
The Parks and Gardens of Cornwall Douglas Ellory **Pett** Alison Hodge 1998
Historic Landscape Survey and Management Plan: Nicholas **Pearson** Associates   Tiverton 2000
Introductory Guides to Pentillie Castle: The Coryton family 2009

Cornwall Record Office: Archivsts summary & introduction;   The Coryton papers, wills, deeds etc.
Peter O'Donoghue, Bluemantle Pursuivant, College of Arms London
Pentillie Estate: Papers and records including estate papers, photograph albums and family collections, plans
Introductory guide to Pentillie Castle: The Coryton family 2009
SCSTyrrell   Personal papers, records and photographs

Thanks are given to:

Wayne Ledley for preparing comparative plans, to Mark Nightingale for setting up the family tree, and to Mrs Kate Tyrrell, Alex Hooper, Dr Joanna Mattingly and the Coryton family (particularly Sammie), for reading the text and making constructive comments.

Illustration credits:

We have tried to trace the origin and owners of all photographs used, crediting the owner where possible. We apologise for omissions or inaccuracies in this list.
The Coryton Family, Ted Coryton, Sammie Coryton, the Pentillie Castle Estate, Rob Partis, Les Spence, Nick Gregory and John Ballard have provided many photographs and these are used with their permission.
All other photographs were taken by S.C.S. Tyrrell from original documents, records or on location.

Author:

Stephen Tyrrell has worked in building restoration for many years. A member of the Institute of Historic Building Consultants, he is enthusiastic about buildings and their history. He still works on the renovation of historic and listed buildings, and also lectures on architectural history.

Recent books include an introduction to the houses and county of Cornwall with drawings by himself. Another of his books *A Visitor in Cornwall* has some 90 watercolours of buildings by Joanna Mattingly and won the *Holyer an Gof* trophy for best illustrated book.

This introduction to Pentillie Castle is the third in a series of detailed guides to the architecture and owners of country houses in Cornwall. Further books in this series and another book on the domestic architecture of Cornwall are in preparation.

His next book on architectural history, the mammoth volume *Early Decorative Plasterwork of Cornwall*, is no doubt eagerly awaited.

Stephen Tyrrell lives near Falmouth with an understanding wife who is still hoping the plasterwork book will be finished soon.